Is China an Imperialist Country?

CONSIDERATIONS AND EVIDENCE

N.B. TURNER, ET AL.

Is China an Imperialist Country?
ISBN: 978-1-894946-75-9

First published by www.red-path.net on March 20, 2014

Readers who wish to correspond with the author, NB Turner, please write to nbturner14@gmail.com

In accord with the wishes of the authors, this text has not been copyedited by Kersplebedeb.

Kersplebedeb Publishing and Distribution
CP 63560
CCCP Van Horne
Montreal, Quebec
Canada H3W 3H8
email: info@kersplebedeb.com
web: www.kersplebedeb.com
www.leftwingbooks.net

Copies available from AK Press: www.akpress.org

Printed in Canada

Whether or not China is now a capitalist-imperialist country is an issue on which there is still some disagreement within the world revolutionary movement. This essay attempts to bring together some theoretical, definitional and logical considerations, and also to cite some of the extensive empirical evidence which is now available, which demonstrates that China has indeed definitely become a capitalist-imperialist country.

We thus approach the question from a number of different angles.

Contents

INTRODUCTION

To friends and comrades, and all who hate imperialism and want revolution, and who believe that Marxism, Leninism, and Maoism must and can become a much more capable and effective force:

It has long been known and understood that the entire world has been under the control of capitalist-imperialism. For a time, a section of this world broke from it, beginning with the victory of socialism in Russia and continuing through the Chinese Revolution, constituting a socialist world. Yet, in time, the socialist countries, through internal class struggles in politics and economics, were seized by capitalist conciliators and advocates, and then by capitalists themselves, who were largely within the ruling communist parties themselves. First in Russia, and later in China, when these counter-revolutions and coups took place, there ensued a period of entry and integration into the world imperialist system. The Soviet Union, at first under the existing signboard of socialism, continued much of its established national and economic power relations into a new social-imperialist bloc (socialist in name, imperialist in reality). The Russian capitalist-imperialist attempt to maintain this bloc, or important sections of what had been part of this bloc, and its historic allies, has continued in the years since the "socialist" signboard was discarded. In China, the defeat of the proletariat and the capitalist capture of state power, after the death of the great revolutionary Mao Zedong, have also led to a period of integration into the world imperialist system. China still operates under a "socialist" signboard, but has conducted itself unambiguously as a capitalist power.

Before the last decade, especially since the demise of the "socialist bloc," the U.S. was commonly seen as the sole Superpower, to which all other powers had to defer. The system which the U.S. had designed, at the end of WW2, was global in scope, and to some more "democratic" in appearance than the old colonial empires. But it was built around the elitist privilege of power and authority, meaning the U.S. as Superpower was at the centerpiece of the controls.

But in the last decade the imperialist world system is not what it used to be. Throughout the world, corrupt and comprador regimes have faced significant and often unprecedented mass popular opposition movements which have revealed the deep instability of the old neo-colonial arrangements. Even in the EU, the product of imperialist designs to supplant the historic internecine battles, there has emerged ever deepening crisis and conflicts, and movements to assert nationalist interests against one another (which can only lead to opposing the EU arrangements overall). Against the "threat" of Islamic fundamentalism, the imperialist system as directed by the U.S. has launched wars such as in Iraq and Afghanistan at huge cost—trillions of dollars, and immeasurable losses in political credibility and imperialist authority, as neither war has won any of the U.S.'s objectives. These clear failures at the hand of the largest and most powerful military force in the world, do not bode well for maintaining the U.S.'s hegemonic domination of the world's imperialist system. And the economic and financial crisis of the last half-decade or more, has stirred not only deep discontent, resentment, and popular political opposition within the ranks of the U.S.'s "reliable" allies, but it has brought to the fore the imperialist anti-U.S. challenges from other major powers—China and Russia. Forces worldwide are studying these changes, and considering how they change the set of options at hand.

The all-too-prevalent view that U.S. imperialism is so powerful, so dominant, and so capable of manipulating all manner of forces and bending them to its will has been, and continues to be, a dangerous twisting of reality. The sole Superpower, in this view, has been attributed with omnipotent features that defy effective challenge, that reflect a supposedly skillful control of contradictions and crises that afflicted earlier empires, and that has a boundless ability to disguise its malevolent work. If it were true, it would be a remarkable development in human history—indeed, it would be, as once touted (in the time of the collapse of the Soviet Union and bloc) by Francis Fukuyama, the End of History (i.e., the end of historical conflict and systemic challenges). It would be an expression of the boastful and fanciful capitalist's post-Mao motto, TINA—There Is No Alternative (to capitalism).

There are others who assert that the U.S. is not so omnipotent, and that it is in decline and may be failing—but that the U.S., and its close allies, constitute the only imperialism that matters, and that, if all—its detractors, victims, opponents, and its imperialist rivals—band together, "liberation" will truly be achieved with the demise of U.S. imperialism. This view also holds that whenever big powers like China or Russia rise in opposition to the U.S., they deserve the support and applause from progressive and revolutionary forces.

Holding this view are a variety of forces who cling to the notion that the Cold War division of the world is still extant and that popular protests in recent years from Libya to Syria, Ukraine and Venezuela (as well as Brazil and Turkey, Iran, even inside western China in Urumqi) are all examples of U.S. meddling and desperate interference. This view holds that without such U.S. manipulation and interference and disruption, the people would, by and large, be happy or passive. This is by any measure an amazing claim, denying the existence of class contradictions and struggles within each of these countries, and making it appear that the conspiratorial powers of the U.S. to manipulate events are unparalleled in reach and effectiveness. In practical political terms, this view distorts the basic reality that many regimes, bourgeois states that usually evoke one (ethnic or religious or nationalist) section of the people over others, aim to repress the sharpening class struggle and broad discontent and rebellion, and a key aspect of that repression is to depict that popular struggle—in diplomacy, media, culture, and in state to state relations—as something else: a defense of national sovereignty against external interference and intervention.

If such claims were valid, there would be evidentiary "smoking guns" produced linking imperial manipulators and local instruments, on the one hand, and at the same time showing that the issues or grievances being protested are false or fabricated/invented, with the foreign hand active in their creation or distribution. To simply say that foreign forces have tried to influence events is always and obviously true—but that they try does not prove they are effective and control events.

The U.S.'s "superpowers" of domination and control are already fading, and the entire world imperialist system is driven to deeper crises and unsolvable contradictions. That capitalism and imperialism are so full of contradiction should not confound proletarian revolutionaries and Marxist-Leninist-Maoists. But many have lagged behind on this understanding in the current world. For some, this is because of the lingering influence and assumptions of past periods, which brought forward the Cold War paradigm and the Third World paradigm and the U.S. Sole Superpower paradigm. These have continued, and become more deeply embedded in progressive and anti-imperialist political culture through the influence of revisionism, of social-democracy, of reformism, of nationalism, of imperialist promotion of pacifism, and pragmatism—amid a broad climate of despair.

The growing conflicts and disputes among imperialist powers, old and new, are but the inevitable seeds of conflict between exploitative and oppressive powers which must expand at each others' expense. All the imperialist powers wish for greater control of the entire world system, but each works with as much as they are able to actually seize. Among revolutionaries, and even among Marxist-Leninist-Maoist revolutionaries, a common illusion continues to be, that the U.S. is the sole enemy, the only Superpower, which possesses such superpowers that only by uniting the people with all who oppose U.S. domination, can the empire be brought down. This has led to political lines which cast class struggles and popular mass rebellions as, actually, an endless series of conflicts between those who assert national sovereignty and national independence against the interference and intervention of external forces commanded (organized, financed, supplied, directed, influenced) by the U.S. This denial of the class struggle, has led to an embrace of local reactionaries and embrace of the local reactionaries' (claimed or real) powerful backers. It has often led to a one-sided opposition to the U.S. and denial that contending imperialist powers are squaring off in a series of "proxy wars" between contending imperialists. And such denials have been made, even by those claiming to be "anti-imperialists."

This line can only develop as a new version of the historically discredited line of "defense of the fatherland" which German socialists adopted before WW1, and which was a large reason for the collapse of the 2nd international. But, in this period, this line takes the form of defending any power "on the outs" or opposed to U.S. imperialism. The historic rejection of this line was sharply and famously opposed by Lenin and the Bolshevik Party which argued for "revolutionary defeatism" toward all imperialist and reactionary powers as the only stance for revolutionaries. They opposed collaborationist nationalism with revolutionary internationalism. And with this line, the October Revolution was won.

In the world today, oftentimes the critics of embattled oppressive local reactionaries are criticized by "anti-imperialists" or "leftists" who say such criticism gives aid and support to U.S. imperialists!

The crisis of the imperialist system is objectively good cause for the advance of revolutionary forces. But the subjective understanding (ideological and political) has not kept pace with the developments in the world, and this can only lead to the irrelevance of internationalist revolutionary proletarian forces, and even prevent their re-emergence as the dynamic force which can lead the process of current widespread rebellion forward to socialist/proletarian revolution throughout the world, and onward to a new future for humanity without national, religious, ethnic, gender, and class divisions—the prospect of communism.

So clarifying the nature of the world imperialist system, its contradictions and cracks and developing contending and opposing powers, is essential for revolutionaries to move forward and lead the organization and ability of genuine revolutionary political forces to seize historic opportunities in the period ahead.

There have been many steps forward in the development of MLM as a world view, an analysis, and methodology. But the development at each turn has depended upon the battle against revisionist distortions and abandonment of basic and time-tested principles and methods. Lenin worked to rescue Marx from the revisionist distortions of Bernstein and Kautsky on the nature of state power (especially the need for the revolutionary overthrow of the capitalist state, in opposition to the line of reformist unity with progressive nationalist unity with the bourgeoisie). Similarly, Mao worked diligently to rescue Lenin from the revisionist distortions of Tito and Khrushchev and Liu Shaoqi (regarding the need to understand and oppose imperialism, uphold proletarian revolution and socialist transformation, and insisting on the independence and keeping initiative in the hands of revolutionary proletarian forces).

The distortions of this period have unique characteristics, but they also repeat many of the historic distortions of Karl Kautsky. There is a neo-Kautskyist view of "ultra-imperialism" that many apply to the power of U.S. imperialism since WW2 to the present. The argument is made that

- the allies of the U.S. are firm, unshakeable and presumably permanent (as far as the eye can see)
- the size and capacity of the U.S. military is, for any would-be challenger, unbreachably overwhelming
- that China is far too much of a "johnny come lately" to be taken seriously as imperialist challenger to the U.S.
- that China has gone from being a comprador and cheap labor resource for the U.S., to a power deeply and critically impaired by being locked into the U.S. financial system, unable to break out
- that there are no potential allies of China (beyond Russia) which could seriously pose the threat of an opposing bloc to the U.S. led-bloc, now or in the future
- that China's military is incapable of posing a military challenge to the U.S., now or in the future
- and even, some argue, there has been a kind of historical maturation to U.S. imperialism (which was previously subject

to the laws of overproduction of capital leading to WW1and WW2) which, since WW2 had sufficient dominance by the U.S., and presumably, sufficient imperialist international architecture, to prevent devastating overproduction crises (and will be able to resolve or control less-than-devastating crises)

- and, some argue, that deep crisis will never lead to inter-imperialist warfare, possibly including nuclear weapons, ever again
- and that such powers and controls by U.S. imperialism and its allies, means that any and all talk of revolution, much less of armed mass revolution, is a fantasy only held by "ultra-leftist" (i.e., not genuine or serious) revolutionaries.
- A variation of this argument holds that pacifist reformism is the only method of genuine change within the imperialist countries.

So, as present-day neo-Kautskyites throw out Lenin and adopt Kautsky, they discard the basics of dialectical materialism and of internationalism and revolution—all in the name of "anti-U.S. imperialism."

It is the responsibility of all revolutionaries to defeat such revisionism, and to clarify the nature of imperialism today, and why revolutionary internationalism must take aim at, and organize forces with clear understanding, that revolution requires opposition to the entire capitalist-imperialist system.

It is with this responsibility in mind, that we offer the following essay on the growth and development of China as a major contending imperialist power in this period. We welcome your comments, criticisms, and suggestions, and we especially encourage further work on this issue. All revolutionary advance in the period ahead requires combating the blinding curse of revisionism. As Mao said, "Cast away illusions, Prepare for struggle!!"

1. What does it mean today to say that a country is an imperialist one?

We Marxist-Leninist-Maoists follow Lenin in our conception of what *imperialism* is in the modern capitalist era. That is to say, we use the term *imperialism* (or what we often also refer to as *capitalist-imperialism,* to be clearer) in a sense somewhat different from the traditional sense of imperialism in the ancient world, or even in the earlier capitalist period.

Imperialism, in this Leninist sense, is *the modern stage of capitalism:*

> "Imperialism is capitalism in that stage of development in which the dominance of monopolies and finance capital has established itself; in which the export of capital has acquired pronounced importance; in which the division of the world among the international trusts has begun; in which the division of all territories of the globe among the biggest capitalist powers has been completed." —Lenin[1]

Note that there have been some secondary changes in the situation since Lenin's time. For example, "international trusts" now generally take the form of Multinational (or Transnational) Corporations (MNCs or TNCs). Similarly, the former direct colonies owned as exclusive preserves by individual capitalist powers are now most often nominally independent neocolonies open to more general predation by all the capitalist power centers. But in its essence Lenin's definition of capitalist-imperialism is still completely valid, and the one we still adhere to.

Lenin also stated that "If it were necessary to give the briefest possible definition of imperialism we should have to say that imperialism is the monopoly stage of capitalism."[2]

Imperialism in the ancient or traditional sense, of being *simply* the domination and economic exploitation of one country by another, is still an essential aspect of imperialism in the Leninist sense. Imperialism, in the narrow sense of a country being dominated and exploited by one or more other countries, in fact *characterizes* modern capitalism as much as monopoly does, and is essential to it. But now there is a lot *more* to what we mean by imperialism. As explained by one recent writer:

> "We Marxist-Leninists seek not merely to describe the political surface of society, but to probe the material underpinnings and bring to light the economic factors and relationships which lead to those political circumstances. Lenin made the choice to use the term 'imperialism' not just to refer to certain political policies of aggression, conquest, and foreign control, but more importantly to refer to an *economic system* that *depends upon such 'policies' for its very existence.* This is a profound new meaning for the term 'imperialism.'"[3]

2. Many Marxists don't fully share Lenin's new conception of imperialism.

But many people, including many who are influenced by Marxism-Leninism, and who may even view themselves as Marxist-Leninists or Maoists, don't really use the term 'imperialism' in the way that Lenin did. They haven't really grasped his conception. They still tend to use the term more in the traditional way, as a reference only to direct military conquest and control rather than to a new stage of capitalism.

Some vaguely Marxist-influenced individuals are quite open about this, such as the "Third World" theorist Samir Amin:

> "Imperialism is not a stage, not even the highest stage, of capitalism: from the beginning, it is inherent in capitalism's expansion. The imperialist conquest of the planet by the Europeans and their North American children was carried out in two phases and is perhaps entering a third."[4]

This is a complete rejection of Lenin's conception, and an insistence on using the word 'imperialism' in its old sense. And in keeping with this, Amin sees only three imperialist centers in the world, the so-called "Triad" (the U.S., Europe and Japan), and refuses to accept that China could possibly be a new imperialist power. For him China has long been part of the "Third World" (or the "periphery" or the "South"), and could never change into anything else.[5] Moreover, views such as those of Amin seem to have had a considerable influence on many others and are promoted by influential forces on the "left" such as *Monthly Review* magazine.

However, a more common sort of view *within* Marxist-Leninist-Maoist circles is to accept Lenin's definition of imperialism in words but to nevertheless still somehow feel that no country can actually be an imperialist one unless it is at or near the top of the heap in terms of military power and frequent engagement in wars of aggression against other countries. That is to say, despite their verbal agreement that imperialism is a stage of capitalism, they still somehow feel that it has more to do with direct and immediate military aggression.

When it is pointed out that there are other countries, such as Japan, Italy and Russia, which are certainly imperialist countries, but which are not at present much engaged in military aggression, they have no good response.* But they still feel in their bones that a country can't really be an imperialist one unless it is like the U.S., and at open war with much of the world. Their central conception of what it means to be imperialist is still the traditional military concept, not the Marxist-Leninist socioeconomic concept of a new stage of capitalism.

* Of course even imperialist countries such as Japan, Italy and Russia (and China—as we will discuss later) have participated in imperialist wars and adventures to *some* limited degree! Post-USSR Russia, for example, has used military force against its southern neighbor Georgia, as well as against internal colonies such as Chechnya and Dagestan. And as we complete this essay, Russia appears to be using its military force to dismember Ukraine.

3. Is the U.S. the "only" imperialist country, or is there an imperialist system?

It is discomforting for some people to think even of countries like Britain, Germany and France as imperialist countries, because—really—when they think of imperialism they are actually only thinking of the United States. The United States ***is*** "imperialism" for some people; they view this as an identity. To oppose imperialism is to oppose the United States. To build a united front against imperialism is to build the unity of virtually all the countries of the world against the United States. Or, if they admit that Britain, Germany and France might be junior partners of the U.S. in its imperial wars, then they still see countries like Russia and China as potential allies "against imperialism". And similarly for murderous local dictators in individual economically underdeveloped ("Third World") countries, such as Saddam Hussein in Iraq, Muammar Gaddafi in Libya, Bashar al-Assad in Syria or the Islamic theocratic regime in Iran, who these people are always trying to find excuses for, or to support outright, in the name of "opposing imperialism".†

And some people who, even in the face of ever-mounting and by now conclusive evidence, finally grudgingly admit that China is an imperialist country, at least according to Lenin's definition, nevertheless still think of China (and often also Russia) as being important forces to ally with. Consider, for example, Jose Maria Sison, the chairperson of the International League for Peoples' Struggle (ILPS). In 2012 Sison denounced the "false claim" that China "is rising as an imperialist rival of the United States".[6] However, more recently still he modified his stance and stated in an interview:

† The International League of Peoples' Struggle (ILPS) under Jose Maria Sison's leadership, and one of the Trotskyist parties in the U.S., the Worker's World Party, are two of the organizations that frequently support such reactionary leaders and their vicious regimes. We must oppose U.S. or other foreign imperialist intervention in these countries, but that certainly does not mean we should in any way support these murderous regimes themselves or refrain from strongly condemning them! It's important to understand this distinction.

> "Indeed, the Dengist counterrevolution resulted in the restoration of capitalism in China and its integration in the world capitalist system. By Lenin's economic definition of modern imperialism, China may qualify as imperialist. Bureaucrat and private monopoly capital has become dominant in Chinese society. Bank capital and industrial capital are merged. China is exporting surplus capital to other countries. Its capitalist enterprises combine with other foreign capitalist enterprises to exploit Chinese labor, third world countries and the global market.
>
> "China colludes and competes with other imperialist countries in expanding economic territory, such as sources of cheap labor and raw materials, fields of investments, markets, strategic vantage points and spheres of influence. However, China has not yet engaged in a war of aggression to acquire a colony, a semicolony, protectorate or dependent country. It is not yet very violent in the struggle for a redivision of the world among the big capitalist powers.
>
> "It is with respect to China's contention with more aggressive and plunderous imperialist powers that may be somehow helpful to revolutionary movements in an objective and indirect way. China is playing an outstanding role in the economic bloc BRICS and in the security organization Shanghai Cooperation Organization beyond U.S. control."[7]

China only "may" qualify as an imperialist country?! Note also in the second paragraph above how Sison seems to still view the acquisition of colonies (or semicolonies, protectorates, etc.) as being essential to imperialism—the way it was *before* World War II. There is something quite outdated in his conception. And note especially how Sison portrays China as a more palatable or acceptable form of imperialism (if it is to be called that at all) which still seems to him to be able to play a positive role in the world! This is tending dangerously close—and may have even crossed the line—to proclaiming "our imperialism" versus "theirs"!

However, it is not just the U.S. imperialists who are the enemy of the people of the world (even if they are at present the strongest and most vicious enemy); *all* imperialist countries are the enemy of the people, and all of them must be opposed. The *entire* imperialist system must be opposed and overthrown! And opposing imperialism should never come to mean supporting local tyrants and local enemies of the people, who, after all, were usually set up as imperialist lackeys and agents in the first place!

The key point that those who hold such views do not understand is that there is *an imperialist system*. The world imperialist system, as it presently exists, is in fact dominated by the U.S., especially militarily. But all the other imperialist countries, including not only Britain, Germany, France, Italy and Japan, but *also* Russia and China, are now part of, and participants in, this imperialist system. All these countries (and even some others, including Holland, Belgium, Canada, Australia and South Korea) benefit from this imperialist system and share in the plunder of the less economically developed countries and in the joint exploitation of the working people of the whole world that this system makes possible.

Everything has a history, and the *world imperialist system* also has a history. It developed out of the old system of quite separate empires consisting of colonies which were the *exclusive preserve* of one or another capitalist-imperialist country. This system proved to be unstable; the colonies kept rebelling and demanding freedom. And new imperialist powers arose (such as the U.S., Germany and Japan) which did not have many colonies, and were thus compelled to try to take some away from the existing empires. This led not only to fairly small wars, such as the Spanish-American War, in which the U.S. stole some of Spain's colonies, but then to two horribly destructive world wars, and even to mass genocide by the Germans in Europe, the Japanese in China, Britain in India (through famine[8]), and the U.S. (via atom bombs) in Japan.

Even from the point of view of the imperialist powers with a lot of colonies there were some serious economic limitations due to the colonial system. While they could keep out other powers from their own colonies, they were in turn kept out of the colonies owned by those other powers. This meant there was an inherent inflexibility in options for the export of capital in the colonial imperialist era, even for the strongest imperialist countries.

So objectively capitalist-imperialism needed to change in a way that would allow a free scope for the worldwide predations by *all* the imperialist powers (operating under agreed upon rules of "fair play") including for new imperialist powers if they arose, and at the same time to grant nominal "freedom" to the colonies. These are the basic reasons why the older-style capitalist-imperialism based on exclusive colonies that existed before World War II was soon transformed into the new world imperialist system based on *neocolonialism** after that war.

The structure of this current world imperialist system had its origins in the "Allied Bloc" of imperialists during World War II. It was not only a military alliance during the war, but also set up international economic agencies (such as the IMF and World Bank) to manage its sphere of control after the war.

Once the Axis Bloc (of Germany, Italy and Japan) was defeated, it was absorbed into this Allied Bloc, which was then usually referred to as the "Western Bloc" (despite the inclusion of Japan). During the state-capitalist period of the USSR and the remainder of the Cold War, there were two essentially independent imperialist systems: the U.S.-led ("Western") Bloc and the Soviet social-imperialist led (so-called "Socialist") Bloc. But after the collapse of the Soviet Union and its satellites, they too were absorbed into the remaining bloc.

However, having now triumphed over almost the entire world, and defeated all its competitors, this was no longer just an imperialist "bloc"; it was now the *world imperialist system*.

China, during the Maoist era, was outside both of the two competing imperialist systems then existing from the late 1950s on. But after Mao's death the capitalist-roaders, led by Deng Xiaoping, transformed China back into a capitalist country, whose ruling national

---

* We are using the term 'neocolonialism' in a broad sense which typically means that the country in question is in effect the collective property of all the capitalist-imperialist powers; sometimes this is also called 'post-colonialism'. We are not using the term 'neocolonialism' in the sense it is occasionally used by some, to mean a country that is a *hidden* colony of a *single* capitalist-imperialist power, such as perhaps the same power which formerly controlled it as an open colony.

bourgeoisie based in the CCP was then faced with the choice to try to develop China separately from the rest of the capitalist world, or to join up and become part of the existing world capitalist-imperialist system. They were compelled to choose the latter course, the only option with any real possibility of success. They "reformed" their own originally state-capitalist economy to a considerable degree along private monopoly capitalist lines†, "opened up" to foreign capitalist investment, and joined the IMF (in 1980), the World Bank (in 1980) and the World Trade Organization (in 2001). They did this with eyes wide open, feeling that they could beat the U.S. and other major powers at their own game, because of China's much greater exploitation of its own vast ocean of very low-paid workers. And so far their gamble has proven to be a great success, as measured by capitalist-imperialist standards (GDP growth rates, trade surpluses, the generation of great wealth for the Chinese bourgeoisie, etc.).

While the U.S. definitely dominated the "Western" imperialist bloc, and has dominated the world imperialist system, its *degree* of domination has been slipping very noticeably over the decades. As we will discuss below, the economic strength of the U.S. (as compared to the rest of the world) has declined tremendously since World War II. Europe's economy is now bigger than the U.S. And now, with the rapid economic rise of China over the past few decades, the U.S. economic domination of the world has nearly ended. Politically and militarily too, the U.S. domination of the world imperialist system is weakening, though more slowly.

Sometimes this is expressed by saying that the once unipolar world dominated by a single superpower has become a multipolar world.

---

† In a later section we will discuss the organization of Chinese capitalism today in a bit more detail. But while it is true that there are still many very important state-owned enterprises (SOEs), it has also become true that these corporations which are officially owned by the state now actually function pretty much the same way as the "private" Chinese corporations do in the national and international market, i.e., as if they were ordinary MNCs. And while Chinese capitalism today still has a stronger state participation in its entire economy (including the private sector) than do most other countries, nevertheless positively *all* capitalist-imperialist countries today can be viewed as a partial merger of the state with the capitalist economy. Moreover, that state intervention and direction is qualitatively expanding everywhere as the world economic crisis continues to develop.

(We will discuss this from another perspective later.) The decline of the United States and the considerable rise of other imperialist powers since World War II serves to further emphasize the importance of viewing contemporary imperialism as a world system, and by no means as the same thing as just U.S. imperialism alone.

It is quite true that the U.S. has been the "world's top policeman" for the Western imperialist bloc since the end of World War II, and for the entire world imperialist system since the collapse of Soviet social-imperialism and its competing bloc in the 1989–91 timeframe. But the U.S. demands that its junior partners also participate in its imperialist wars (such as in Iraq and Afghanistan), and this need is further intensified because the economic weakening of the U.S. is making it ever more difficult for the U.S. to hold this world imperialist system together through its individual military might. And countries such as France and Britain often, and increasingly, take the lead in "maintaining order" (in a way that benefits all the major capitalist countries as well as themselves) in their smaller former colonies in Africa and elsewhere.

However, *all* the major capitalist countries greatly benefit from the military "policing" still carried out or directed mostly by the U.S. This policing is not just for the U.S. alone, but also on behalf of the entire imperialist world system. All these major capitalist countries, now including Russia and China, also participate in the economic penetration and exploitation of not only the less developed countries but are also allowed to invest in and operate exploitative corporations within each others' borders. China's current huge push into Africa, for example, is enabled because the U.S. (with the aid of Britain, France and others) is keeping the continent open and available for economic penetration and exploitation by all the capitalist powers.*

But you might ask: If the U.S. is doing most of the military fighting,

---

* We could also mention in this connection the U.S. military's AFRICOM command, which has placed military advisors in many African countries; the significant role played by the French imperialists in "stabilizing" the Ivory Coast, Mali and other countries, and in bringing down the Gaddafi (Quaddafi) regime in Libya; and the development of a few countries such as Nigeria as regional cops sometimes working in the service of the world imperialist system.

or at least directing or controlling it, to maintain the world imperialist system, why then does it "allow" all these other major capitalist countries to share in the plunder? There are two main answers to this:

1) The U.S. recognized long ago that despite its great military power it could not hold the world imperialist system together all by itself. Unless other principal capitalist powers were allowed to benefit from the system they would oppose it, undermine it, and seek to build competing imperialist blocs and spheres of control, which might even lead to additional world wars. And in order for the U.S. to secure the right to sell to and invest in other leading capitalist countries, it has had to create international rules which allow those countries to also sell to and invest in America. (Furthermore, its bourgeois *economic ideology* erroneously maintains that every country will benefit more or less proportionally from such a system, and since it was the biggest it thought it would always benefit the most. And its *political ideology* favored the neocolonial method of world exploitation because it didn't have many colonies itself!)

2) The U.S., in leading in setting up this world imperialist system, arranged for some very special benefits for itself that the other countries do not share. For example, it has a grossly disproportionate share in the control of the international institutions that were set up (especially the IMF and the World Bank). Even more importantly, the U.S. dollar was granted a special status in this world imperialist system. Initially this was because the U.S. owned most of the gold bullion in the world at the end of World War II, and the dollar was made convertible into gold. But even after President Nixon ended this (because the U.S. was rapidly being depleted of gold), the dollar still had a special status as the primary international reserve currency. Basically the U.S. has had the right since the end of World War II to just print dollars and buy the products of the world with them!† (However, in recent decades more and more constraints have devel-

† This remains a major irritation to other imperialist countries. For example, in a recent "leader" (editorial) the *Economist*, a leading publication of the British ruling class, noted that "America enjoys the 'exorbitant privilege' of printing the world's reserve currency." [Oct. 5, 2013, p. 11.]

oped on this ever-more-reluctant munificence of the rest of the world toward the U.S. Moreover, the euro has now become one alternate reserve currency and there are predictions that the Chinese renminbi (or yuan) might someday soon also become an international reserve currency.[9])

So, yes, the U.S. has provided the primary military force to maintain this world imperialist system, but it was not just out of the "goodness of its heart"! It has gotten paid for doing this, and paid handsomely! Think of it this way: There has been a division of labor among a group of international gangsters. The chief enforcer has been the U.S., but the other gangsters have mostly been willing to have it this way since they have also benefitted tremendously from the arrangement. And the U.S. has been "willing" to share in the plunder both because it had to, and because it got a much bigger and more stable share of the loot by doing it this way.

4. China as an integral part of the world capitalist-imperialist system.

The deal to bring China into this international capitalist-imperialist system required China:

- To continue its already existing economic transformation back to capitalism at home, and to make a commitment to mostly do this along Western monopoly capitalist lines. (State monopoly capitalism was to be more and more cut back, or made nominal, which China was already doing anyway.)
- To (more or less) fully open up its economy to foreign investment by MNCs based in other countries, and allow them to also exploit local low-paid Chinese labor both for the Chinese market and for export.

- To (more or less) play by the international rules of this world imperialist system, including the rules promulgated by the IMF and WTO.

In exchange, China was:

- Granted membership in the WTO and access on nearly equal terms to the international markets for its goods. Unequal tariff barriers and such were qualitatively lowered.
- In a much better position to acquire foreign technology, not only in foreign factories operating in China, but also in locally owned Chinese factories.
- Allowed to export capital to other countries in the world imperialist system, to buy up foreign mines and other companies which are a major source of raw materials needed by the Chinese economy, and to set up subsidiaries of its own corporations (state owned or private) in foreign countries, and to buy up assets all around the world.

As this arrangement developed, and China became ever more important in the world economy, there was a tacit financial agreement tacked on top of this: China would be allowed to run a huge trade surplus provided that it used a large part of this surplus to buy up a great part of the ever-growing government debt that the U.S. and other countries were incurring. The present world economic system could not continue functioning if this was not happening. (It is highly unstable, even as it is!)

So not only is China an integral part of the world capitalist-imperialist system, with its ruling class benefitting tremendously from its participation in this system; this world system has in turn become overwhelmingly *dependent on China* for its crucial role within it: Both its huge role as a manufacturer of low cost goods, and its critical role as a lender to the U.S. and other countries to prop up the whole international financial system. China is now not only part of the world imperialist system, its economic and financial role within that system has become as essential as America's military role!

China's economy is now not only certainly a capitalist economy, but a *monopoly capitalist* economy. And because its state-owned enterprises (SOEs) now operate much as if they were private multinational corporations, it is from a Leninist standpoint unambiguously also an imperialist country. (Remember: Capitalist-imperialism in the modern era *is the same thing as* monopoly capitalism, according to Lenin!)

5. Foreign investment in China does not preclude its being an imperialist country!

It is often argued that China can't possibly be an imperialist country because foreign imperialist countries such as the United States have investments in China and are exploiting ***it!*** The idea seems to be that you must either be the victim of imperialism or the country doing the victimizing, but that you can't be both!

Since the beginning of modern capitalist imperialism well over a century ago, the imperialist powers have always exported goods to each other's countries; have always purchased or set up factories in each other's countries; and have always exported capital to each other's countries, and have thus always exploited each other's working class. In fact, the *largest* part of their export of capital is actually to other imperialist countries (even if this is *not* usually the *most profitable* part). And this has especially been true for those countries which did not have a lot of colonies themselves. Moreover, the percentage of what is known as "cross investment" in each other's economies by the imperialist powers has generally increased over time.[10]

In talking about the export of capital, in 1916 Lenin said:

> "How is this capital invested abroad distributed among the various countries? *Where* is it invested? Only an approximate answer can be given to this question, but one suffi-

cient to throw light on certain general relations and connections of modern imperialism.

> "The principal spheres of investment of British capital are the British colonies, which are very large also in America (for example, Canada) not to mention Asia, etc. In this case, enormous exports of capital are bound up most closely with vast colonies of the importance of which for imperialism we shall speak later. In the case of France the situation is different. French capital exports are invested mainly in Europe, primarily in Russia (at least ten billion francs). This is mainly *loan* capital, government loans and not investments in industrial undertakings. Unlike British colonial imperialism, French imperialism might be termed usury imperialism. In the case of Germany, we have a third type; colonies are inconsiderable, and German capital invested abroad is divided almost evenly between Europe and America." —Lenin[11]

Thus even in the period before World War I a considerable part of the export of capital from imperialist countries was to other advanced capitalist and imperialist countries!* After World War I this trend intensified.† And after World War II this trend intensified vastly more. World War II destroyed a tremendous amount of productive capital

---

* In another place Lenin notes, in criticizing Sokolnikov for his view that the export of capital *always* results in superprofits: "It is difficult to accept as correct the statement on superprofits and new countries since capital has also been exported from Germany to Italy, from France to Switzerland, etc. Under imperialism, capital has begun to be exported to the old countries as well, and not for *super*profits alone." [From "Revision of the Party Programme" (Oct. 6–8, 1917), in "Lenin on Imperialism and Imperialists" (Moscow: Progress, 1973), p. 129.]

† In the volume *New Data for V. I. Lenin's 'Imperialism, the Highest Stage of Capitalism'*, published by International Publishers in the late 1930s, we find:

> "*Important changes in the direction of capital exports.* First of all, Russia has dropped out as a sphere of investment and as a source of super-profit. Secondly, Germany has now entered the list of countries which import capital. The technically and economically most advanced country in Europe has now become a source of super-profit obtained from capital exports." [p. 293]

in Europe and Asia, and this opened up the possibility for the export of capital to those countries on a much greater scale. By far the largest target for the export of U.S. capital after that war was none other than the major imperialist countries of Europe (i.e., to Germany, Britain, France and Italy)!

And has the fact that the U.S. and other countries have exported huge amounts of capital to those countries in any way prevented them from being imperialist countries themselves? Certainly not! In the very same way, the fact that the U.S. and other imperialist countries now export capital to China, and set up factories there, in no way shows that China is not also now a major capitalist-imperialist country.

What single country has been the greatest destination for the export of capital? In recent decades, up through 2011, it was none other than the United States itself!* We take it for granted that no one would use this fact to conclude that the U.S. is not an imperialist country.

Moreover, while other imperialist countries export capital to China (and to each other), China in turn also exports capital to those countries. And substantial amounts of it, too. In fact in 2012 about *one-third* of China's foreign investment was to the advanced capitalist countries of Europe.[12] China's investment in Europe has hugely increased in part because of the continuing economic crisis there, which opens up *opportunities* for China and *necessities* for financially strapped European companies and countries.† In addition China exports a great deal of capital to the U.S., Canada, Australia, and other advanced capitalist countries. In total, about two-thirds of China's outward direct investment in 2012 went to these rich countries, up from just a tenth in 2002.[13] (We will talk more about this later.)

---

* In 2012, for the first time, and mostly because of a big drop in FDI going into the U.S. that year, China surpassed the U.S. as the favorite target for foreign direct investment. (Data sources are provided in in endnote 65 on page 159.)

† Europe is coming to depend more and more on China to help bail it out of its crisis, not only in severely depressed countries like Greece and Spain, but even elsewhere. For example, the Chinese auto giant Dongfeng has just agreed to purchase part of the ailing French automaker PSA Peugeot Citroën for $1.1 billion. [*San Francisco Chronicle*, Feb. 20, 2014, p. C-2.]

Another point to consider is that while "inward foreign direct investment" (IFDI) into China, and outward FDI (OFDI) from China to other countries, are both still growing, the rates of growth of OFDI are now much higher than the rates of growth of IFDI. That is, the trend is now for the ratio of outward bound investment to inward bound investment to increase. In the first 4 months of 2013, for example, inward FDI into China increased by only 1.21% (as compared to a year earlier), while outward FDI from China to other countries increased by 27% over the same period.[14]

6. Can new imperialist countries arise in the world today?

Sometimes it is argued that given the stranglehold of the world by the existing capitalist-imperialist powers, *new* capitalist-imperialist powers cannot possibly arise. However, the facts say otherwise.

The original leading capitalist-imperialist power was Britain. But during the latter part of the 19th century the new capitalist-imperialist powers of the United States, Germany, France and others all arose along with Britain, and despite its initial dominance. Early in the 20th century the new capitalist-imperialist power Japan arose, and Russia was also transformed from an old-style imperialist power into a fledgling capitalist-imperialist power (though with internal rather than external colonies).

Was that the end of the story? Of course not. Other imperialist powers have also developed over this period. And Italy, already an imperialist country by then, invaded Abyssinia (Ethiopia) in 1935–36 and turned it into a colony.‡

‡ Italy was already an imperialist country by World War I and joined the side of the British-French-Russian Entente in large part in order to expand its territory. In 1935–36 it conquered Ethiopia and in 1939 it annexed Albania which had been a de facto protectorate for decades.

Then in the 1950s the once socialist Soviet Union, when it and the Communist Party of the Soviet Union were captured by a rising new state-bourgeoisie from within, also became a new capitalist-imperialist country. Mao appropriately called it a *social-imperialist* country, a country still hanging onto the "socialist" sign-board (until 1991), but in reality a new imperialist country.*

This historical experience demonstrates very clearly that new imperialist powers can in fact arise in the modern era, even in the case of countries that were once actually socialist! It also demonstrates that a country which is partly state-capitalist (or even almost entirely so—as the Soviet Union was) can be an imperialist country just as much as one which is organized along the lines of private monopoly capitalism of the Western variety.

Although the social-imperialist Soviet Union was—alongside the U.S.—a superpower, it never "replaced" the U.S. as the world's most dominant imperialist country. Rising new imperialist countries do not necessarily supplant existing imperialist powers.

In 1916 Lenin wrote that "Capitalism is growing with the greatest rapidity in the colonies and in overseas countries. Among the latter, *new* imperialist powers are emerging (e.g., Japan). The struggle among the world imperialisms is becoming more acute."[15]

In the early years of the 20th century too the dominant imperialist powers "had a stranglehold" on the world, and yet it was still possible for new imperialist countries to arise. It is a totally unsupported

---

* This is not the place for any extensive discussion of the social-imperialist Soviet Union, nor even to decide when, exactly, it could be said to have first become an imperialist country. It could be argued that the USSR became an imperialist country as soon as the new bourgeoisie seized control of the CPSU and government in the 1950s, since it already had political dominance over other Eastern European countries and immediately began exploiting them for the benefit of its own new ruling class. Or, as some argue, the Soviet Union only emerged as a full-fledged imperialist country around 1968 when it acted aggressively—invaded Czechoslovakia—and when Brezhnev promulgated his theory of "limited sovereignty" for the countries the Soviet social-imperialists had dominance over. The precise timing of this change is not that important; what is most important for us here is that this development of the Soviet Union as an imperialist power, and it along with its bloc as an imperialist system, did in fact happen.

dogma that this "cannot" happen, and that it "cannot" have happened in the case of China more recently.

In some respects it is actually *easier* for a new imperialist power to arise in the post-World War II era in which capitalist-imperialism has become a world system. The export of capital, for example, can now begin without the necessity for a rising imperialist country to first conquer other lands militarily and then turn them into exclusive colonies, or else to first steal colonies from established imperialist powers through inter-imperialist warfare.

One of the objective reasons why the old colonial version of capitalist-imperialism had to be replaced by the newer neocolonial imperialist system was to set up the rules for all imperialist countries—including newly arising ones—to participate in the exploitation of the people of the world, and especially those in the more undeveloped countries. Moreover, the expanded horizon for the international liquidity of capital was a key motive for this new post-World War II imperialist architecture.

7. The size of the Chinese economy today.

China's economy has rapidly expanded ever since the 1949 revolution (with only a few short-term interruptions). It expanded rapidly during the socialist era,* and it has continued to expand rapidly even since China was transformed back into capitalism (though now for the primary benefit of the few and not the many). It is hard to compare the statistics from the two periods, but it is possible that China's economic growth has even speeded up somewhat since the return of capitalism, at least during the last decade or two.†

Marxists have never denied that in many circumstances capitalist economies can rapidly expand. In the *Communist Manifesto* Marx and Engels emphasize this rapid productive growth potential under capitalism to a degree that even pro-capitalist readers find startling!

However, is this still true *in the imperialist era?* Yes, sometimes it still is! Lenin said that capitalism in the imperialist era is characterized by

* In particular, China's socialist economy expanded at a very rapid pace during the Great Proletarian Cultural Revolution (often dated from 1966 through 1976), averaging more than 10% per year! See: Mobo Gao, "Debating the Cultural Revolution: Do We Only Know What We Believe?", *Critical Asian Studies*, vol. 34 (2002), pp. 424–425; and Maurice Meisner, *The Deng Xiaoping Era: 1978–1994*, p. 189. Even the capitalist-roaders themselves had to admit that, except for brief declines during the Great Leap Forward and the first 3 years of the GPCR, the growth of both industrial and agricultural production during the rest of the Maoist socialist period (1969–1976) was very fast. See the charts on the second page of the article "China's Industry on the Upswing", *Beijing Review*, Vol. 27, #35 (Aug. 27, 1984), p. 18ff., online at: http://www.massline.org/PekingReview/PR1984/PR1984-35.pdf The later claim of the capitalist-roaders that the Cultural Revolution was a "disaster" for the economy was an outright lie. Even the brief production declines of the first three years of the GPCR were very rapidly made up for beginning in 1969, and the overall trend line from before the decline and after it was as if the short decline had not even occurred!

† Figure 7.1 below in this section shows that during the first 10 or 15 years of the return to capitalism the share of China's fraction of world GDP actually declined. But since then it has zoomed up tremendously. This suggests that China's GDP growth rate in the socialist era was fast, that it may have slowed down relative to the rest of the world for the first part of the new capitalist era, but then has become very fast again during the past 20 years.

stagnation and decay, and overall that certainly seems to be correct as the current economic crisis is demonstrating anew. Nevertheless, there was a major world capitalist boom in the quarter-century after World War II, and Germany and Japan had especially powerful booms. This was because of the massive destruction of productive capital during that war (and the accompanying cancellation of consumer and state debt) which cleared the ground for a new boom.

A boom in newly capitalist China was also possible, in part because there was virtually no state and consumer debt load from the socialist era. So, in other words, the normal situation under capitalist-imperialism is indeed for there to be stagnation and decay (or worse!), but this may not apply for a while to new capitalist-imperialist countries nor to countries which have gotten a "fresh start" because of the massive destruction of capital and debt in a devastating world war. (And despite the deaths of millions of people.)

In the modern era of capitalist-imperialism, at least from the early 20th century on, it has for the most part proven to be quite impossible for economically undeveloped countries to break out of this condition and seriously begin to develop their economies in a major, sustained and all-round way—*except through socialist revolution* (as in the case of Russia and China). It is true, as Lenin noted, that the export of capital to economically backward and low-wage areas does serve to promote the development of capitalism there to some degree. But that development remains mostly in the hands of foreign corporations (MNCs), and in a form that serves to primarily promote the extraction of wealth from the undeveloped country. Independent local capitalist development in these countries is choked by the stifling domination of foreign imperialist countries and their MNCs.

However, there have been a very few exceptions to this general rule which require explanation. A few countries in East Asia, and South Korea most prominently, have managed to develop their economies even under the capitalist system. At the end of World War II, when Korea was split into two countries by the U.S., North Korea was much more developed industrially than the South—which was largely agricultural. But since then South Korea's economy has developed in a truly major way until now the country actually qualifies as an advanced capitalist country. It is too far from our central topic to thoroughly explore how this was accomplished (let alone what happened to North Korea!). But we believe the basic explanation is that the two dominant foreign imperialist powers in South Korea (namely the U.S. and Japan) purposely promoted the independent development of a capitalist economy there as part of their geopolitical necessity to halt the advance of "Asian Communism". For example Toyota, the Japanese auto company, gave tremendous help to the South Korean corporation Hyundai to build its auto division into a successful car company, even though this meant creating a major competitor to Toyota and the other Japanese auto companies! This sort of foreign tutelage and the limits forced on foreign MNCs operating in South Korea (by allowing the South Korean government to establish effective protective tariffs for example*), allowed a national bourgeoisie to emerge in the country and develop its own locally-based economy.

Something similar, though on a less impressive scale, was allowed to happen by the U.S. and other imperialist powers in Taiwan and a few other "Asian Tiger Economies",[16] and for the same reason: To build up their economies to try to prevent the spread of "Communism". But there are serious constraints on allowing this sort of unfettered development generally since this would have a very negative impact on the profits of the MNCs of the major imperialist powers. In any case, the Asian Financial Crisis of the late 1990s began to show the limits of such capitalist development and the current more general

---

* The use of means such as protective tariffs may *help* develop a country's capitalist economy—*given that* they are allowed by foreign imperialism to establish and maintain those tariffs and other measures! Lenin criticized Bukharin (who promoted protective tariffs) by saying "that no tariff system can be effective in the epoch of imperialism when there are monstrous contrasts between pauper countries and immensely rich countries". ["Re the Monopoly of Foreign Trade", (Dec. 13, 1922), *Lenin's Collected Works* 33:457] However, Lenin did apparently make his argument in too absolute a form as the quite exceptional case of South Korea seems to show. In that rare situation the foreign imperialist powers controlling the country decided that it was actually in their interests to allow local development in South Korea in order to build up a bulwark against "Communism", and therefore allowed an effective tariff system to be put in place.

crisis is likely bringing the initial "success" of this type of capitalist development near to an end.

The bigger exception we need to discuss, to the general rule that undeveloped (or "Third World") economies cannot develop in a sustained and complete way under capitalism, is the case of China itself. How is it possible that China's economy has continued to develop so tremendously since the transformation of socialist China back to capitalism?

There are two aspects to the answer to that question: First, China was no longer really "undeveloped" at the time of Mao's death; on the contrary, it had already made major advances in the independent development of its economy during the period of socialism. Second, and even more important, the new Chinese bourgeoisie which captured power after Mao's death was itself independent of foreign imperialist control.

In China's case, the necessary political independence to promote the locally based development of its newly capitalist economy only came about because of its earlier socialist revolution and period of socialist development.† During this socialist period there was a complete political break from foreign imperialism, and this political independence in China largely continued *even after* the restoration of capitalism. In other words, the new ruling class in China was basically

† This is the persuasive position of Fred Engst in his essay "The Rise of China and Its Implications", July 9, 2011. Engst argues that this political independence must in turn promote a period of independent economic development:

> "Contrary to neoclassical theory, Chinese development shows that in the stage of imperialism, if a country wants indigenous economic development under capitalism, it first needs to break from imperialist domination so that it can have a period of independent development before entering the worldwide capitalist system. Otherwise, its own economy will be suffocated by the multinationals under the aggression of imperial powers."

We would, however, disagree with the possible implication here that it might make sense for a country attempting to develop to try to first implement a temporary period of socialism, and then purposely end it and switch back to capitalism in a supposed stronger position! What happened in China was a specific historical case, with its own particularities, and is by no means a general recipe for economic development! (We think that Fred Engst would agree with us on this point!)

a bureaucratic national bourgeoisie, and not a comprador bourgeoisie. Of course there are some compradors in China, just as there are in every country, but they are not the leading core of the ruling class.*

So the notion of some, that further economic development in China could only continue if China remained socialist, was incorrect. In April 1976, while Mao was still alive, a much more sensible view was published in *Peking Review.* The article recognized that even if the proletariat lost control of the country the Chinese economy might still develop, but that if it did so "it would turn out to be modernization of an imperialist or social-imperialist type."[17] And this is exactly what has actually occurred.†

It did appear to many that with Deng's "opening up" of the Chinese economy to foreign MNC investment the new bourgeois ruling class in China had become compradors. But this was a superficial view, a misperception, which did not get at the essence of the situation. The "opening up" was in fact a step toward integrating China's largely independent economy into the world capitalist economy, but for the conscious purpose of further promoting China's own national economy and its own bureaucratic national bourgeoisie centered in the CCP.

However, what that old article in *Peking Review* said is certainly true: The complete and sustained modernization and development of any economy in the imperialist era can only be done either through socialist revolution or else (in very special circumstances) in an imperialist manner. In China's case it was through socialism for a few decades and in the imperialist way since then.

---

* In other words, the presence of compradors—agents expressing foreign capital's interests—does not define the *social system* as "comprador" unless these compradors are a ruling core capable of subordinating other national interests to foreign interests.

† And in this connection it is worth recalling Mao's criticism of Deng Xiaoping: "This person does not grasp class struggle; he has never referred to this key link. Still his theme of 'white cat, black cat,' making no distinction between imperialism and Marxism." [Quoted in Chin Chih-po, "Denial of the Difference Between Socialism and Capitalism Is Not Allowed", *Peking Review* #16 (April 16, 1976), p. 18. Online at: http://www.massline.org/PekingReview/PR1976/PR1976-16e.htm]

Figure 7.1: Share of World Nominal GDP (%)[18]

	U.S.	CHINA	JAPAN	GERMANY	FRANCE	BRAZIL	U.K.	ITALY	RUSSIA/USSR	INDIA	CANADA
2012	22.5	11.4	8.3	4.8	3.6	3.3	3.4	2.8	2.8	2.5	2.5
2011	21.6	10.5	8.4	5.1	4.0	3.5	3.5	3.1	2.7	2.6	---
2010	22.9	9.4	8.7	5.2	4.0	3.4	3.6	3.2	---	2.7	2.5
2005	27.6	4.9	10.0	6.1	4.7	1.9	5.0	3.9	---	---	2.5
2000	32.0	4.1	12.8	5.9	4.2	1.7	4.6	3.5	---	---	2.2
1995	24.8	2.5	17.9	8.5	5.3	2.6	3.9	3.8	---	---	2.0
1990	26.2	---	14.1	7.8	5.7	2.1	4.6	5.2	3.2	---	2.7
1985	33.7	2.5	11.0	5.7	4.4	1.8	3.7	3.5	---	1.8	2.9
1980	25.2	---	9.7	8.4	6.3	---	4.9	4.2	---	---	2.4
1975	28.0	2.8	8.7	8.2	6.2	2.1	4.1	3.8	---	---	2.9
1970	35.6	3.2	7.3	7.3	5.1	1.5	4.3	3.8	---	2.1	3.0
1965	38.8	3.6	4.7	---	5.2	---	5.2	3.5	---	3.0	2.8
1960	38.4	4.6	3.3	---	4.6	1.1	5.3	3.0	---	2.7	3.0

Source: World Bank statistics from a table of the top 10 countries each year posted on Wikipedia, except for the 2012 figures which are based on GDP estimates by the IMF. The figures for China exclude Hong Kong, Macau and Taiwan. Nominal GDP is GDP calculated at official exchange rates, and is not adjusted for inflation. Note that the figures fluctuate from year-to-year due to booms and recessions in different countries, but that over longer periods overall trends can still be discerned.

Figure 7.2: U.S. & China — GDP Comparison for 2012[21]

	NOMINAL GDP		GDP IN PPP EQUIVALENT	
	AMOUNT (BILLIONS)	% OF WORLD GDP	AMOUNT (BILLIONS)	% OF WORLD GDP
U.S.A.	$16,244.575	22.49%	$15,684.80	18.34%
CHINA	$8,221.015	11.38%	$12,470.98	14.58%

Not only has China's economy grown very rapidly in absolute terms over the past six decades, it has even rapidly grown as a percentage of world production—while the other major capitalist-imperialist countries, and especially the U.S., have all declined in these percentages.

Looking carefully at Figure 7.1 on the previous page, we see that over the past half century the portion of world GDP created in a given year in the U.S. has dropped from over 38% to 22.5%, a very substantial decline. (Immediately after World War II the U.S. share of the *capitalist world's* total industrial production was 56.4 percent![19]) Japan's share of world GDP rose steadily until it reached its peak in 1994, and then began to decline. The shares of world GDP of Germany, France, Britain and Italy also rose greatly after World War II, but have now declined noticeably over the last decade and a half. In recent years only China, and to much smaller extents Brazil and India, (of the major countries shown in this chart) have substantially increased their share of world GDP. In 1990 China was not even in the top 10 countries in terms of world share of GDP, but now it has surpassed Japan, Germany, France, the U.K., Italy and Russia to take the number two spot in the world, behind only the U.S.

However, there is a better (truer) measure of the real share of world production that countries have than what is shown in Figure 7.1. This alternative uses not GDP figures translated into dollars on the basis of official currency exchange rates at the time, but rather a translation into dollars based on the equivalent purchasing power of the local currencies within their own country. This is called the Purchasing Power Parity (PPP) conversion rate.[20]

Figure 7.2 shows what a huge difference it makes if you translate China's GDP into dollars using the PPP conversion rate rather than the currency exchange rate. Either way, China's GDP has been rapidly gaining on the U.S. over the past few decades. But China's economy is still only about half the size of the U.S. economy if nominal GDP comparisons are made, while it is now nearly 80% the size of the U.S. economy if PPP conversion rates are used!

Most economists studying the world economy now believe that China's economy will surpass the size of the U.S. economy quite soon.

If PPP conversion rates are used (as they really should be) some predictions are that China will surpass the U.S. as early as 2015 or 2016! Even if nominal GDP conversion rates are used, it may only be 5 to 10 years until China's economy surpasses the U.S.

Another point to consider is that the U.S. economy is artificially inflated in size because of the grotesque parasitism of the service and especially the financial services sector. If you look only at the basic core of the economy (i.e., manufacturing) China has now virtually matched the U.S. if it has not already exceeded it. (Figure 7.3 below only shows the statistics up through 2009.)

In this graph we see that while the U.S. share of world manufacturing value added has over the past 40 years dropped from over 26% to around 20%, China's has jumped from around 1% to at least 18%. Moreover this calculation, once again, was done by translating Chinese figures into U.S. dollars at the prevailing currency exchange rates. If instead the more truthful PPP conversion rates were used then China would definitely have already well overtaken the U.S. in its share of world manufacturing value added.

Figure 7.3: U.S. & China — % of World Manufacturing[22]

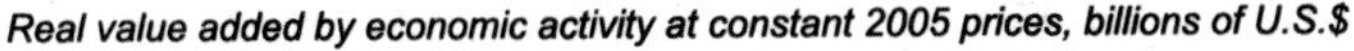

Real value added by economic activity at constant 2005 prices, billions of U.S.$

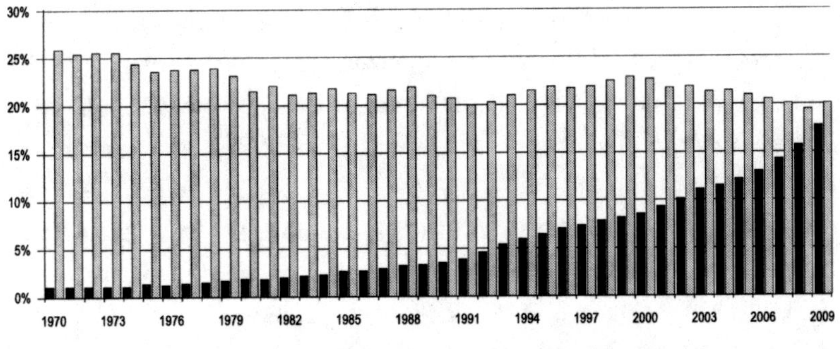

U.S. Manufacturing as % of Total World Manufacturing

China Manufacturing as % of Total World Manufacturing

Source: United Nations National Accounts database
http://unstats.un.org/unsd/snaama/resQuery.asp

Whether China has the largest *overall* economy in the world in terms of GDP (as it almost certainly will have soon), or only the second largest economy in the world (as it already has at present), can it be seriously imagined that a country with a capitalist economy of this magnitude and importance—*and in the capitalist-imperialist era when capitalism itself has become capitalist-imperialism!*—can be anything but a capitalist-imperialist country?!

Note that almost all the other major capitalist economies in the world today, including not only the U.S., but also Japan, Germany, France, Britain, Italy and Russia are clearly imperialist countries. How could China, the second largest and the fastest growing capitalist economy, not also be an imperialist country in this capitalist-imperialist era?? How could you even call this era the imperialist stage of capitalism if one of the most important capitalist countries is not considered to be an imperialist country? It just wouldn't make any sense!

We should not leave this topic about the size and rapid growth of the Chinese economy without briefly mentioning the fact that a very large part of China's population has benefitted either very little, or else not at all, from this enormous growth. As with capitalist growth in any country, and certainly for the world as a whole, the new wealth created has mostly gone to the few.

What was once, in the Maoist era, one of the most egalitarian countries in the world has become one of the most unequal—with the contrast between rich and poor becoming ever more extreme.

Economists have a measure they call the "Gini coefficient" to measure inequality. A Gini coefficient of zero means that there is no inequality whatsoever, while a coefficient of 1 means the most extreme inequality possible (one person having everything and everybody else having nothing at all). So the lower the Gini coefficient the more equal the society. In the world today there are no truly egalitarian countries, but the Gini coefficient for personal income in Sweden is 0.23 and in Germany is 0.27. For a highly unequal country like the U.S., with its dozens of billionaires and many millions of poor people, the Gini coefficient in 2009 was a very large 0.468.

In China the Gini coefficient has been getting bigger and bigger for decades! In 2001 it was 0.40, in 2007 it was 0.415 and in 2012 it reached 0.474, which is even worse than the U.S. despite including the notorious "1%" (the very rich) alongside the mass of people struggling to get by.[23]

Thus the massive and rapid economic growth in China is mostly benefitting the ruling bourgeoisie which is getting ever richer. It is true that there has developed a fairly large "middle class", but nevertheless (and as the growing Gini coefficient demonstrates) this is a very secondary process to the overall continuing polarization of wealth.

Moreover, in China there is the continuing exploitation of the working class, when they can find jobs at all. There is quite massive and growing unemployment. There is the super-exploitation in factories of many tens of millions of migrant workers from rural areas, and serious discrimination against them. There are very widespread land grabs by local government officials and real estate developers. There are many forms of continuing discrimination against women. There is national oppression and discrimination against minorities. There is the fact that genuine unions are illegal, as are most democratic rights such as free speech, freedom of the press and freedom of assembly. There is a growing environmental catastrophe in progress, with air and water pollution reaching crisis levels. There are millions of people without access to health care and other social benefits such as sick pay and retirement income.

So when we speak of the Chinese boom we should always remember that no matter how big and fast it is, it is for the most part not for the benefit of the hundreds of millions of workers, peasants and ordinary people in China. That is simply impossible under capitalism.

8. Monopoly and Finance Capital in China.

Earlier we quoted Lenin's definition which says in part that "Imperialism is capitalism in that stage of development in which the dominance of monopolies and finance capital has established itself…" So have monopolies and finance capital established dominance *in China* today? They certainly have! And, moreover, this overall dominance is not by *foreign* monopolies and *foreign* finance capital, but clearly by Chinese monopolies and Chinese finance capital.*

During the Mao era, when China was a socialist country, industrial production was consolidated and centrally directed through overall socialist planning. When Deng Xiaoping and his cohorts transformed China back into capitalism after Mao's death, all these industries initially remained state owned and the economy was, to begin with, almost entirely state capitalist. Over time, and especially during the 1990s, many of these "state-owned enterprises" (SOEs) were privatized, and many additional private companies and corporations were established and grew. And with the "opening up" to foreign investment, many foreign corporations also began to set up factories and operations in China, mostly for the export of commodities produced with cheap Chinese labor.

What this has all meant is that in the new capitalist era state capitalism in China has been considerably (though still only partially) transformed into *private* monopoly capitalism. Of course state capitalism itself is a form of monopoly capitalism in the general sense—and even a more concentrated and further monopolized form of it! And even if China had retained near total state capitalism, as the Soviet Union did in its last 35 years, it would have still been an imperialist country. But the fact that China has partially switched over

* We should note, however, that since Lenin's day a new term has been introduced, namely 'oligopoly', which is—strictly speaking—more correct than "monopoly" which often implies *total* or *complete* monopoly. 'Oligopoly' is semi-monopoly, or a "looser form" of monopoly. In other words, a situation where a small number of producers control the capitalist market for some commodity and limit their competition, generally to matters of styling and advertising.

to Western-style private monopoly capitalism has made its form of capitalist-imperialism look more similar to that in the U.S., Europe and Japan.

Even though China has been a capitalist country for decades now, as of 2012 SOEs still make up about half of the economy in terms of assets owned and about one-third in terms of value-added production. About 20% of Chinese employees work at these SOEs, down from 60% as recently as 1998. (See chart.)[24]

However, it should be understood that these many remaining Chinese state-owned enterprises (SOEs), though they do in fact constitute a type of state capitalism from a formal perspective, now actually operate much more as if they were privately owned monopoly corporations. Some of the first significant steps in this direction were taken in the economic "readjustment and reforms" of 1979 when SOEs were "granted some decision-making powers, such as [over] the distribution of profits".[25] A different sort of bourgeois "reform" of SOEs, beginning in the early years of Deng Xiaoping's return to

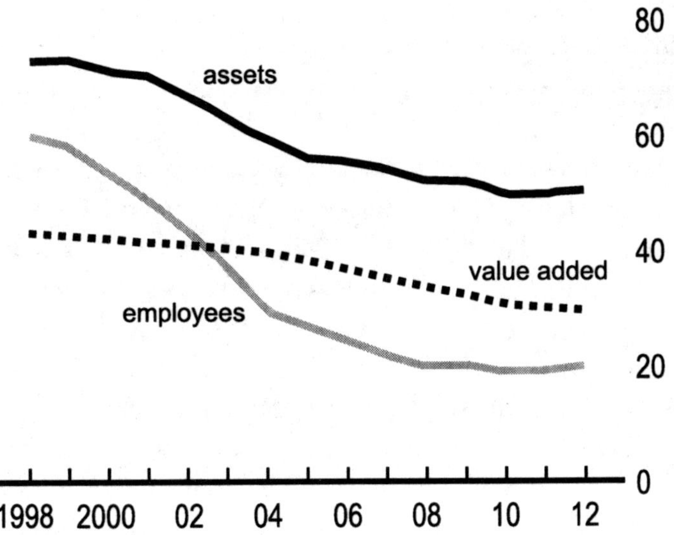

power after Mao's death, was the dismantling of the "iron rice bowl". In the Maoist era, workers in state enterprises were guaranteed permanent employment status, an eight-hour day, an eight-grade wage scale in which workers could move up through seniority, free medical benefits, pensions, paid maternity and sick leave and subsidized food, housing and childcare. With the return of capitalism all these benefits have been stripped away and are no longer obligations of SOEs. One of the motives of the new bourgeois ruling class for closing down so many SOEs, other than low profitability, was the strong outrage of the workers to the loss of these benefits and the growth of serious labor unrest because of this. In some cases the government just had no choice except to shut down some enterprises entirely, given their exposed and hated new management policies.

Another big step in changing SOEs to be more like private corporations was made with the new regulations for SOEs introduced in May 1984, which stated (among many other things) that "businesses have the right to produce whatever is needed or is in short supply, after fulfilling their state plans and orders", set prices themselves (within ranges), choose their own suppliers, decide their own staffing (hiring and firing), adopt any wage system they like (including piece work), etc.[26] And in the decades since then the management of SOEs has time after time been granted ever freer latitude to operate their corporations pretty much as they wish, and focusing primarily on the production of profits. The biggest change, of course, occurred when definite state production plans were abandoned, with the shift to a market economy.

While capitalist China today still has loose overall five-year plans to help coordinate its economic development, these plans no longer specify exactly what goods each SOE should produce, or how many of each commodity, what the prices should be, etc. On the contrary, these SOEs are now nearly as free as private corporations are to make their own decisions about what and how much to produce, how much to charge, when and where to expand, etc. It is now the dictates of the *capitalist marketplace* which are the primary determiners of what SOEs produce, not any socialist production planning, and further emphasis is continually being put on allowing markets to play the "decisive role" in the allocation of resources.*

Moreover, in China even privately-owned monopoly capitalist corporations are under somewhat more state/Party direction (or "interference", as they often view it) than occurs in Western capitalist countries. (Of course, in the capitalist-imperialist era there has been a partial merger of the corporations and the state everywhere, to varying degrees, as Lenin pointed out—see sidebar next page.) So the difference between SOEs and private corporations in present-day capitalist China is not nearly as great as one might imagine. Both types of formal ownership are tools for the exploitation of the Chinese working class by the ruling capitalist class. And *both* types of formal ownership represent the *partial* merger of the capitalist state with semi-independent units of production, though to somewhat different degrees.

One important reason why the state and Party in China have more influence over private capitalist corporations than is common in other capitalist-imperialist countries is that the owners and managers of these private corporations are often themselves members of the CCP! A very large number of such "red capitalists" have joined the CCP over the past dozen years.† A second group of "red capitalists" were already in the CCP when they became capitalists! In 1992 the CCP began encouraging members of the Party to start their own

---

* This "decisive role" for markets is the terminology used in the communiqué of the Third Plenum of the Eighteenth Central Committee in November 2013. Previously the market was described as merely the "basic" determiner of the allocation of resources. The change in terminology—though slight—was meant to put yet further emphasis on market forces. See: "The Party Plenum: Everybody who loves Mr Xi, say yes", *Economist*, Nov. 16, 2013, p. 49.

† In 2001 General Secretary of the CCP Jiang Zemin lifted the ban on capitalists joining the "Communist" Party. The ideological justification for this move was his theory of the "Three Represents"—i.e., that the CCP should represent not only the workers and the peasants but also a third group which included businessmen, professionals and others. The CCP planned to admit 200,000 managers or owners of large or medium-sized private businesses as new Party members by 2002. Many more such "red capitalists" have been admitted since then, though the figures have not been released—presumably because they are politically sensitive. [Bruce Dickson, *Red Capitalists in China* (2003), especially pages 102–104.]

Lenin refers to "the beginnings of state-controlled capitalist production, combining the colossal power of capitalism with the colossal power of the state into a single mechanism and bringing tens of millions of people within the single organization of state capitalism" in his article "War and Revolution", May 1917, in *Lenin's Collected Works* 24:403. However, it should be remembered that the role of the state in directly guiding the capitalist economies of the major imperialist countries tremendously increased during World War I, and that after the war was over this direct role was severely cut back again. Moreover, the term "state capitalism" came to have a qualitatively different (and deeper) sense once the formerly socialist Soviet Union became state capitalist in the 1950s.

Nevertheless there are any number of mechanisms by which "private enterprise" and the state are blended together even in the West. For example, there is the fact that corporate wealth and the rich and their media largely determine who gets elected to political office; there is the fact that corporate lobbyists largely determine the details of new laws; there is government regulation of corporations (direct and indirect, such as through tax laws) and also "regulatory capture", wherein corporations supposedly being regulated by government agencies gain control over the regulatory bodies (through bribes or otherwise); and there is the "revolving-door syndrome" ("cronyism") whereby government officials (or even industry regulators!) become corporate managers (and vice versa) [see http://www.sourcewatch.org/index.php/Government-industry_revolving_door and http://www.thenation.com/article/174151/reverse-revolving-door-how-corporate-insiders-are-rewarded-upon-leaving-firms-congres].

private business operations. This is what became known as *xiahai*, or "plunging into the sea" of private enterprise. These *xiahai* capitalists were acting on Deng Xiaoping's well-known admonition that "to get rich is glorious", and they have generally kept their membership in the CCP in order to maintain their political connections and influence. As of 2002 roughly one-fifth of China's private entrepreneurs were already members of the CCP, and two-thirds of them were *xiahai* capitalists.[27] Some of China's biggest "red capitalists" now appear on the Forbes list of the world's billionaires!

With the "opening up" to foreign investment in China, foreign MNCs quickly came to generate a very large percentage of the manufacturing production in China *that was exported to other countries.* (Indeed, one of the primary purposes of this "opening up" was to foster this development.) In 1995 exports from foreign-funded enterprises in China were 31.51% of total exports; in 2003 they reached 54.84% of total exports; and in 2008 they topped out at 55.25% of total Chinese exports.[28] This domination of Chinese *exports* by foreign-funded enterprises led some people to erroneously conclude that foreign MNCs were dominating the entire Chinese economy. There are several things to consider in coming to understand why this is simply not the case.

First, since 2008, while the *value* of exports by foreign-funded enterprises has continued to rise, the *percentage* of total exports coming from foreign-funded enterprises has been gradually *falling*. Chinese government statistics showed that this percentage had fallen to just below 50% in 2012.[29] Moreover, while exports from SOEs in 2012 dropped by 4.1% from a year earlier, and exports from foreign-funded enterprises rose by 2.8%, the rise in exports from privately-owned Chinese companies increased by a much larger 21.1%.[30] The trend now is therefore for locally-owned private Chinese companies to take over an ever-larger part of the export market.

Second, many of what are counted as "foreign-funded enterprises" in Chinese statistics are not really foreign! In particular, Hong Kong based companies are included in the "foreign-funded" category even though Hong Kong has actually been part of China since 1997. Moreover, Hong Kong is by far the largest single source of "inward foreign direct investment" into China, accounting for $456.2 billion (or 41%) of accumulated "foreign" inward direct investment as of 2010.[31] This compares to an accumulated FDI from the U.S. of only $78.7 billion (7.1% of the cumulative total) as of 2010.

Many people have somehow got the idea that the Chinese economy is dominated by Western imperialist countries such as the U.S., Britain and Germany, but it just isn't so. Even if you add together the accumulated inward FDI (as of 2010) from the U.S., Britain, Germany, France and Japan it only comes to $197.4 billion—which is much less than half of that from Hong Kong alone![32] And there is also quite a bit of investment from Taiwan, South Korea, Singapore and even tiny Macau (which is also now part of China), none of which can possibly be considered as a foreign power capable of bossing China around or controlling its economy.

Third, even the export component of the Chinese economy is itself declining in importance over time. The Chinese government is making an ever more determined effort to reduce its economy's reliance on exports, and major changes have already been made in this direction. The exports of goods fell from 38% of China's GDP in 2007 to just 26% in 2012.[33] The *value* of Chinese exports continues to rise, but the internal Chinese economy is growing much faster. This is why the *percentage* of Chinese exports as a part of total GDP is falling so fast.

Therefore the notion that foreign imperialist countries and their MNCs dominate the Chinese economy is quite erroneous, as is the sometimes accompanying notion that foreign imperialism controls China politically.

Things are even clearer and more obvious when we look at the financial heights of the Chinese capitalist economy. All the big banks are under tight control by the government and Party. As the British ruling class magazine, the *Economist,* noted in reference to China, "The country's biggest financial institutions are so closely held by the state that they are, in effect, arms of the treasury."[34]

Four of the ten largest banks in the world are now Chinese, including the biggest of them all, the Industrial and Commercial Bank of China (ICBC) which has assets of $2.8 *trillion*! The other three are the China Construction Bank ($2.2 trillion in assets), the Bank of China ($2.0 trillion), and the Agricultural Bank of China ($2.1 trillion).[35] These banks are the core of Chinese finance capital and are under careful and attentive direction by the government and Party. "The sheer size of these institutions is breathtaking. ICBC and ABC have over 400,000 employees each, nearly as many as Volkswagen, the world's biggest carmaker. ICBC has over 4 million corporate clients. CCB has some 14,000 branches."[36]

One Western book about China's financial sector, and representing the views of foreign financial capitalists, laments that China's "central government has unshakable control of the sector", adding that "foreign banks hold, at best, little more than two percent of total financial assets" and "despite the undeniable economic opening of the past 30 years and the WTO Agreement notwithstanding, China's financial sector remains overwhelmingly in Beijing's hands."[37]

The "Big Four" banks are led by senior figures in the CCP hierarchy, "with bosses shuttling easily between banks and regulatory agencies."[38] This state control of the big Chinese banks is very important in many ways. It is one of the primary mechanisms that allow the government and the Party to supervise the entire economy and to arrange for stronger investment in the parts of the economy it chooses to strengthen or promote. And loans to SOEs have been especially promoted. This is one of the reasons that the state-capitalist sector of the Chinese economy has remained as large as it is.

This sort of overall control of the economy by the financial sector is true to a large extent in all imperialist countries in the capitalist-imperialist era, and is the reason that this financial sector is at the very center of what is called "the commanding heights" of the economy.* This is partly why Leninists so strongly stress the concept of financial capital. But in China this financial command is not in the hands of Wall Street profiteers as it is to a considerable extent in the U.S., but is

* The very term "commanding heights" of the economy comes from notes prepared by Lenin in November 1922, for a speech at the Fourth Congress of the Comintern. See: *Lenin's Collected Works* 36:585; online at: http://www.marxists.org/archive/lenin/works/1922/nov/13b.htm

instead directly in the hands of the "ruling committee" of the Chinese bureaucratic national bourgeoisie centered in the CCP.

Nevertheless, these giant Chinese banks are themselves extremely profitable, to the point of being the great envy of other major banks around the world. ICBC alone had pre-tax profits of nearly $50 billion in 2012.[39] In late 2012, China's four largest banks reported a combined third-quarter profit of 150 billion yuan ($30 billion), almost triple the amount made by the top four U.S. banks during that same period.[40] "Bank profits as a share of China's economic output equaled nearly 3% last year [2012], whereas the highest ratio achieved in recent decades by American banks was only 1% of GDP (in 2006)."[41]

Following the path of the Western world's giant banks in this age of financial capitalism and globalization, these giant Chinese banks are now expanding their operations globally. There have been obstacles in doing this in many countries because these state-owned Chinese banks do not follow all Western banking standards and do not wish to fully open their books to foreign eyes. However, Chinese banks are making progress in sidestepping such difficulties. On a trip to China in October 2013 George Osborne, Britain's Chancellor of the Exchequer, announced an agreement to allow Chinese state-owned banks to operate in London by classifying them as branches rather than subsidiaries, and thus avoiding rigorous scrutiny. International trading in the Chinese yuan has tripled over the past three years to $120 billion per day, and London wants to secure its position as the center of this huge and growing trading in Chinese currency, and also in Chinese bonds, by allowing Chinese banks to operate there.[42]

The response of foreign imperialists to the rapid rise of these big Chinese banks has been in two opposite and conflicting directions. On the one hand, they are impressed, envious (especially of the big profits) and fearful of this new competition. In a review of one very recent book glorifying American giant banks and strongly opposing any attempt to cut them down to size so that they are no longer "too big to fail", the *Economist* summarizes one of the author's primary conclusions: "Trimming them [the big U.S. banks], he frets, may lead to 'a point when America can no longer be called a super power' and would be 'handing the baton to China.'"[43]

On the other hand, a popular theme in Western bourgeois economic literature is that China's banks are in a "fragile" condition. These banks are viewed as being too much under CCP political control and thus too ready to make loans to Chinese companies that those companies will not be able to pay back. There is of course some truth to this, but what these critics fail to understand is that absolutely *all* capitalist financial systems *everywhere* do this very same sort of thing! And *must* do so!

Bourgeois economists cannot admit, and few of them can even understand, that the creation of credit bubbles is absolutely essential to *every* capitalist boom in *every* country. The reason is simple: Capitalism inherently involves the extraction of surplus value from the working class. Since the workers are not paid for all the value they produce, they cannot possibly buy back all that they produce—unless they are granted ever larger amounts of credit. If consumer credit is expanded, the market for commodities is expanded. And in that case the expanding market makes it possible for corporations to use part of their surplus value, or else to borrow from banks, to build more factories to sell to that expanding market.*

And this is exactly what every capitalist boom amounts to. In reality it is a house of cards which must eventually, and inevitably, collapse in the form of an overproduction crisis brought to a head by one or more financial crises. And yes, this will inevitably happen in China too, at some point.

But because there was no internal or external debt in China during the socialist period[44], the room for the creation and expansion of credit in the new capitalist era has been much greater than in the U.S., Europe or Japan, which were already wallowing in mountains of debt built up over the decades since World War II. *This* is the primary rea-

* The major variation on the theme is when consumer credit can no longer be expanded fast enough. In that case, in the capitalist-imperialist era governments themselves take on the necessary debt, by either borrowing money from the rich, or else by just printing it. These "Keynesian deficits" can prolong booms for an additional period, though in the end the joint debt bubble of consumer and government debt must still eventually pop.

son why China has so far been much less affected by the world overproduction crisis and its attendant financial crises; they simply have had the ability to increase their credit/debt load in a much greater and faster way. Thus, in relation to the sizes of their economies the stimulus packages during the 2008–9 financial crisis were much greater and much more effective in China than elsewhere.

A related view common in the Western bourgeois economic literature about the Chinese financial system is that it has been leading to a "gross misallocation of capital". Well, of course from a Marxist point of view this is also inevitable under capitalism, and there have been many especially absurd examples which can be pointed to. In the U.S. in the late 1990s, for instance, there was the so-called "New Economy" or "Dot.com" boom, wherein there were massively disproportionate (and totally unwise) investments in Internet companies, some of which never made a profit at all. Many billions of dollars were lost in such foolishness. Following that collapse in the recession of 2000–2001, a new wave of misallocation of capital in the U.S. began in what turned out to be major housing bubble and the securitization of bundles of subprime mortgages. That too collapsed (or partially so) in 2008–2009. A similar sort of thing happened in Japan in the late 1980s, with the grotesque real estate bubble that collapsed in the early 1990s. What, indeed, is a capitalist boom if not a "gross misallocation of capital"—which only becomes fully clear when the bubble bursts?

The Chinese financial system does in fact have many problems which are continually building up, just as are those of all the other capitalist-imperialist countries. There is certainly a housing bubble building up in China, for example.* There is a shadow banking system in China, just as there is in the U.S. (though it has a somewhat different character). There is quite a lot of overproduction presently evident in China (as elsewhere). There are some new "ghost cities"

* This housing bubble in China has been building up for many years. In 2013 the sales of new homes exceeded $1 trillion for the first time. The total value of new home sales rose by 27% from a year earlier, while average new home prices in December 2013 rose by 16% in Beijing (from a year earlier), by 18% in Shanghai, and by 20% in Guangzhou and Shenzhen. ["Housing: Sales in China top $1 trillion", *San Francisco Chronicle*, Jan. 21, 2014, p. D2.]

with thousands of apartments and offices currently unoccupied. All these things and many more are true.

However, this is in the very nature of capitalism for there to be a lot of economic anarchy of this sort, and for there to be expanding debt and asset bubbles during boom times. None of this shows that Chinese capitalist-imperialism is fundamentally different from other capitalist-imperialist countries.

9. "Expansionism" and "Sub-imperialism".

But if China is an imperialist country now, then how about India and Brazil? How about South Africa, South Korea and Australia? Where do we draw the line, and how?

And if *capitalism itself* has really been transformed into a new *imperialist stage* over the past century and more, does that mean that positively *all* capitalist countries are now also imperialist countries?!

Obviously not! Here is the sensible way to resolve this supposed conundrum: The ruling classes of all capitalist countries in the capitalist-imperialist era operate in the same imperialist way to *the extent that they are able to do so!* But most are not able to do so to any significant degree. For example, it would be totally absurd to think of Haiti, Nepal, Cambodia or Mali as imperialist countries, regardless of how bourgeois and ambitious their ruling classes are, and despite the fact that there are a tiny few extremely rich capitalists even in countries like this who individually benefit from the world imperialist system.

In Nepal, for example, which is one of the poorest countries in the world, there is just one billionaire, Binod Chaudhury, who not only has a large business operation in Nepal but who has actually built a global conglomerate business operating in 45 countries.[45] Chaudhury benefits from the world imperialist system, and is a participant in it. But Nepal as a whole is nevertheless a victim of world imperialism, and its ruling class parties (including a couple major parties which absurdly still call themselves "Marxist-Leninist" or even "Maoist"!*) are largely subservient to foreign imperialism and Indian expansionism.

The ruling classes of most countries in the world today are forced into the position of being compradors (or de facto agents) of foreign imperialist powers, and of the world imperialist system as a whole, to a very considerable extent. (For a limited time they can also forge partnerships with international capital, but such arrangements are always transitional.) If they become too independent, if they seek to promote their own national economic interests in opposition to the interests of international imperialism, then tremendous economic pressure is put on them, sometimes rising to the level of outright economic warfare. And if they persist they are apt to suffer serious political interference and even assassinations or political coups engineered by foreign imperialist intelligence agencies. And, if all that still doesn't whip the recalcitrant local ruling class back into line, the world imperialist system will mobilize its massive military forces (usually at present led and/or organized by the U.S.) to invade the country and forcibly attempt to set up a new client regime friendly to the world imperialist system.

However, if the capitalist ruling class in *any* country today becomes powerful enough, that is, if that country develops a sufficient level of economic and military strength, it will become more and more internally independent of other powerful capitalist-imperialist countries. Its ruling class, which originally had no choice but to more or less be compradors to some powerful foreign imperialist countries (or to the extremely powerful imperialist system as a whole) will more and more start to take on *some* of the characteristics of a national bourgeoisie working more exclusively for its own class interests, and in growing contradiction to the interests of other bourgeois ruling classes in other countries. It will begin to take advantage of

---

* We are referring to the so-called Communist Party of Nepal (United Marxist-Leninist) and the so-called Unified Communist Party of Nepal (Maoist), both of which are now not only engaged in social-democratic parliamentary politics but are also clearly subservient to the Indian ruling class and the world imperialist system. There are also other nominally Marxist-Leninist or Maoist parties in Nepal whose genuine revolutionary nature has yet to be demonstrated.

the existing world imperialist system to also export capital and join in the exploitation of the rest of the world—even if its own working class and natural resources continue to be exploited by other powerful foreign countries too.

For most small countries in Asia, Africa and Latin American this can simply never happen to any significant extent; they can never hope to become imperialist powers. But for some few countries like India and Brazil it has started to happen in a very partial way. It is not correct to view these countries as no longer being exploited by foreign imperialism, or as having become full-fledged imperialist countries themselves. Quite the contrary, their major aspect is still as countries dominated and exploited by foreign imperialism. Their ruling classes remain primarily compradors, even if they are also starting to occasionally engage in independent action and focus somewhat more on their own national class interests and goals (see sidebar on next page).

Revolutionaries in South Asia appropriately describe the Indian ruling class as "expansionist".† This means that the Indian ruling class seeks to dominate the entire South Asia area (and perhaps eventually the entire Indian Ocean basin and beyond). This sort of expansionism is really a junior sort of local imperialism. It involves the same forms of economic penetration and military dominance as imperialism at the world level does. The top imperialist countries do not really mind that India does this (at least within limits); in fact they often encouraged and lauded it! It seems only natural to the top imperialist countries that regional sub-bosses should emerge and help "keep order" there, along with some "acceptable" level of regional looting. Clear examples, among many others, include the Indian support for

† The term "expansionism" for India derives from the terminology used by Maoist China to criticize India's territorial claims and military actions against China (over border disputes) and similar claims and actions against other neighboring countries, and the doctrines of the ruling class in India which led to these actions: "These reactionary expansionist ideas of India's big bourgeoisie and big landlords form an important part of Nehru's philosophy." —"More on Nehru's Philosophy in the Light of the Sino-Indian Boundary Question", by the Editorial Department of *Renmin Ribao* (Oct. 27, 1962), English translation in *Peking Review*, #44, Nov. 2, 1962, pp. 10–22. This specific quote is on p. 11. Available online at: http://www.massline.org/PekingReview/PR1962/PR1962–44.pdf

Marxists have often supposed that there is a sharper opposition between the comprador bourgeoisie and the national bourgeoisie in a "Third World" country than there really is. They sometimes view these two sections of the ruling class as totally distinct and totally opposed to each other. It is generally not like that at all!

In the case of India, to give a specific example, it is sometimes falsely supposed that there are two very opposed sections of the ruling class, the comprador bourgeoisie and the bureaucratic national bourgeoisie (dominated by families such as the Tatas and the Birlas), and only *one* of these sections holds true political power (namely, the compradors). The other section, representing the Tatas and the Birlas, is supposedly too weak to gain real power. But imagine that somehow (if only as a thought experiment) a political party representing *only* the national bourgeoisie (and *not* the "compradors") were to come to power in India. What really could they get away with doing differently than what the current regime is doing? The real issue is not what these different sections of the ruling class may *want to do now,* or which section is supposedly dominating the country, but rather what the *entire* ruling bourgeoisie in India is *forced to do* at the present time by world imperialist financial and political realities, whether they like it or not!

Moreover, even compradors normally have hopes of eventually becoming independent of foreign imperialism, and of developing as a national bourgeoisie themselves. If India somehow does manage to rise as a real imperialist power in the future it will not be because the Tatas have defeated the compradors; it will be because the Indian ruling class as a whole gradually changes from being largely a class of compradors into largely a national bourgeoisie because of the broader changes in the political and economic possibilities that develop for that ruling class (which would be contingent on ending the primitive constraints of feudal relations in the country as a whole).

It is mostly only in the context of rapidly expanding social revolution and complete national crisis, when one part of the national bourgeoisie might actually decide (for tactical and for self-preservation reasons) to support the revolution, where we have the really serious conflict between these sections of the ruling class that people are familiar with because of the history of the Chinese Revolution.

the repressive state of Sri Lanka, the domination of Nepali resources, and providing troops for the U.S. occupation of Afghanistan.

Thus Indian expansionism is itself an aspect of the current world imperialist system.

In the same sort of way the Brazilian bourgeoisie has been seeking to play an ever-more regionally dominant role, economically and politically, in South America. Brazil, like India, now exports some capital to other countries (even beyond its own region and to Africa especially), though each is also the recipient of much larger capital inflows.*

We could say that there are signs that the ruling classes of India and Brazil are taking on *some* of the characteristics of a national bourgeoisie, even though they remain most essentially bureaucratic comprador bourgeoisies so far. They are clearly sometimes struggling against their constraints, as when they join with China and Russia in such schemes as setting up a BRICS bank independent of the U.S., Europe and Japan. (More about this below.)

Is it possible that some day India, Brazil, and perhaps even a few more countries, might graduate from the status of mere expansionist (or "sub-imperialist") countries and become full-fledged imperialist powers themselves?

Well sure, this is conceivable, sometime in the future. But we must be clear that this is not at all the case today. India and Brazil are in a qualitatively different situation than is China in the present world economy and power structure.

---

* Actually the situation is somewhat different in Brazil than in India. According to an OECD chart of Foreign Direct Investment Outflows, during the 5 years from 2008 through 2012 India had total outward FDI of $71.7 billion, while Brazil had total outward FDI of just $18.2 billion. Moreover, in 3 of those 5 years (including 2011 and 2012) Brazil actually had *negative* outward FDI (i.e., some of its previous outward FDI was eliminated through sale, losses, repatriation, etc.). For comparison purposes, during this same 5-year period China had total outward FDI of $262.9 billion, Russia had $220.0 billion, and South Africa had just $5.2 billion (also with 2 negative years). This information comes from the OECD document "FDI in Figures", April 2013, Table 2, online at: http://www.oecd.org/investment/statistics.htm The *inward* FDI for these and other countries is shown in Table 1 of that same report.

A few words about the term "sub-imperialism". This term can be used in various different senses, including:

(A) As a reference to countries such as Britain, France, Germany, and Japan, in relation to the single U.S. superpower. However, this conception downplays the imperialist nature of countries other than the U.S., and therefore implicitly supports the erroneous idea that there really is just one imperialist country and not a world imperialist system.

(B) As a reference to countries which serve primarily as regional agents for the major imperialist powers (the U.S., Britain, France, Germany, Japan, etc.) and for the world imperialist system. South Africa has frequently been referred to as "sub-imperialist" in this sense, since it has often intervened in other countries in southern Africa on behalf of international imperialism and with their backing. And India and Brazil could also be considered "sub-imperialist" in this sense.

(C) As a reference to a few countries (especially India and Brazil) whose ruling classes have serious imperialist ambitions themselves, are showing somewhat more political independence from the existing powerful imperialist countries, and are starting to take on some characteristics of a national bourgeoisie rather than as a mere comprador bourgeoisie as in the past, and whose countries are starting to export capital. This is the sense of the term "sub-imperialism" that comes closest to meaning a form of junior or want-to-be imperialism. (And what a despicable goal that is!)

In our view, sense (A) is quite wrong and should be completely opposed. Sense (C) makes the most logical sense. However, sometimes authors use the term "sub-imperialism" in a rather ambiguous way, blending the (B) and (C) senses.[46]

Calling countries like India and Brazil "sub-imperialist" today does seem quite reasonable. But if we do so we must be sure to keep in mind that this does *not* mean that they are now full-fledged imperialist countries, but merely that their ruling classes have dreams of becoming such, and are presently just beginning to show some limited independence from the established imperialist countries. Their abilities (and need) to export capital and demonstrate independent military strength are still fairly small.

Perhaps because of the possible confusion of senses of the term "sub-imperialism" many revolutionaries seem to prefer to use the existing term "expansionism" instead, since it is already well-established, especially in South Asia.

In summary, in the modern era the basic form that capitalism itself takes is monopoly capitalism or imperialist-capitalism (with the degree of state participation in the economy varying considerably, however). But the individual ruling classes in the world are either near the top of this dog-eat-dog system, or near the bottom. Only a very few are intermediate, with some visible characteristics of each. Historically some few countries have graduated from the bottom ranks of countries which were primarily exploited by more powerful capitalist countries, and have become primarily exploiting imperialist countries themselves. Most recently this has clearly happened in the case of China. Whether it will happen to a few other major capitalist countries, such as India and Brazil, is an open question. At present, however, this still seems doubtful, especially in light of the major world capitalist economic crisis that is still in its fairly early stages and yet is developing inexorably.

10. The present world imperialist system is NOT a form of "ultra-imperialism"!

The present world *capitalist-imperialist system* is *not* really the total domination of the world by a single superpower, even though it is very often erroneously assumed to be that. It is in reality a temporary club of convenience of international gangsters, with one long dominant but now steadily weakening leader, which will begin to break part to some substantial degree if it becomes advantageous for one or more significant countries or sections within it to bring that about.

Just as the current imperialist system had its origin in multiple imperialist blocs, it will surely break apart anew into at least somewhat separate and hostile competing blocs eventually. Why is this? It is for the very important reason that Lenin put his finger on so long ago: the inevitable uneven development within capitalism and within the capitalist-imperialist system—and the unending objective of capitalism to expand (or die) at each other's expense.

Lenin noted that this uneven development is characteristic of capitalism in general and at all levels of organization: "Uneven and spasmodic development of individual enterprises, of individual branches of industry and individual countries, is inevitable under the capitalist system."[47] But he also pointed out just *why* this uneven development especially occurs once capitalism reaches its imperialist stage, and needs to export capital in search of new sources of profit:

> "The export of capital affects and greatly accelerates the development of capitalism in those countries to which it is exported. While, therefore, the export of capital may tend to a certain extent to arrest development in the capital exporting countries, it can only do so by expanding and deepening the further development of capitalism throughout the world." —Lenin[48]

Lenin also pointed out that "Finance capital and the trusts do not diminish but increase the differences in the rate of growth of the various parts of the world economy."[49] Today we might well rephrase that as: "Finance capital and *multinational corporations* do not diminish but increase the differences in the rate of growth of the various parts of the world economy." They do this by searching the world for the places to invest which promise the highest rates of profit, and shifting more capital to those regions. And of course super-profits are to be made where the wages are especially low, but where the necessary infrastructure and trained and disciplined labor force is fairly well developed, or rapidly developing. China has fit these requirements almost precisely, and that's an important reason why both state and private monopoly capitalist development in China, both foreign owned and locally based, has been booming for several decades already.

The relative *political* stability of the world imperialist system since the collapse of the Soviet Union has depended on the more or less stable *economic* relationships of the U.S. and other major capitalist countries. But it is a law of capitalism that different countries and regions will develop economically at different speeds and to different degrees. Some will advance, and some will decline, either relatively or sometimes even in absolute terms.

In particular, the U.S. has been seriously declining in relation to the other elite members of the imperialist club since that club was set up at the end of World War II. As we saw in the last section, the U.S. share of world GDP has dropped from about 50% at the end of World War II to 22.49% in nominal GDP terms, and to only 18.34% in GDP-PPP terms in 2012. In the past decade or two the closest allies of the U.S. in the imperialist system club (principally Britain, France, Germany and Japan, as well as a number of others) have also been declining economically. Meanwhile Russia is recovering somewhat from its horrendous economic collapse with the fall of the Soviet Union in 1991. Most importantly, China has been zooming forward in its economic expansion for six decades now. And a few more countries, especially the "expansionist" or "sub-imperialist" countries India and Brazil, are now expanding their economies (though in quite distorted forms) and are becoming a little bit more independent too. All this is changing the world balance of economic power at a surprisingly fast pace in historical terms.

In the mid-1800s Britain was known as the "workshop of the world". But that changed. By the early 1900s the main workshop of the world was the United States, and Germany had also surpassed Britain. Now manufacturing is in serious decline in the U.S.[50] and everyone appropriately views China as the main workshop of the world. As the world changes it is necessary for our ideas to change along with it.

Military power follows economic power, though with a substantial lag. As China gets stronger economically and the U.S. declines economically, the present huge advantage in U.S. military strength will gradually diminish. The U.S. is already having tremendous and increasing difficulties prevailing in the endless series of imperialist wars it is waging in the "Third World". And the huge expense of these endless wars is proving to be very damaging to the U.S. fiscal situation, and is leading to even faster increases in its financial indebtedness to China. (This is reminiscent of how the great cost of colonial wars and World Wars I & II speeded up the decline of British and French imperialism.)

The rise of China and the decline of the U.S. will lead to a much more serious economic struggle between them, and quite possibly a bifurcation of the present single imperialist system into two competing blocs, and even the eventual possibility of inter-imperialist military struggles between them (probably via proxy wars, etc.). We will talk some more about increasing U.S.-China contention later.

All these changes will be speeded up and become more contentious because of the continued development of the world overproduction crisis.

We should make it clear that when we talk of imperialist "blocs" we are not necessarily talking about *war blocs!* Blocs of nations are more typically, and over the longest periods, *economic blocs.* This is why the main issue at present is not really about the relative military strength and capabilities of the different arising blocs, but rather about their current and future economic strength. On the other hand, in extreme circumstances economic blocs also develop into war blocs.

Consequently, while it is true that there is now, and has been for two decades, a single *world imperialist system,* this is not at all the same thing as "ultra-imperialism". Nor is having a *single* world imperialist system something that will likely continue in place as long as capitalist-imperialism continues to exist. Capitalist-imperialism is just not that stable!

11. BRICS as a sign of internal strain within the present world imperialist system.

BRICS is an acronym for five important countries which have been gaining in economic power in recent years: Brazil, Russia, India, China and South Africa. Of these, China has by far the largest economy and the fastest rate of economic growth.

However, all of these countries are somewhat outside the main centers of world *political* power. Russia and China were once socialist countries; Russia had a long economic and Cold War struggle with the U.S. and its allies (with hard feelings and distrust still remaining*); and Brazil, India and South Africa have all had a long history of imperialist domination and exploitation. So there is history of these countries clinging together to some degree in challenging the U.S.-led imperialist system from within. "BRICS" has become not only a convenient way of referring to some nations which are, as a collective whole at least, rising in economic power, it has also been moving in the direction of becoming a more formal conference or even a tentative international association of these 5 countries, in the midst of certain contrary pressures and internal strains among its members.

As mentioned earlier, the World Bank and the International Monetary Fund, which were set up at the close of World War II by the U.S. and its allies, gave the U.S. a grossly disproportionate share of the voting rights and control of these institutions. This has not set well with the BRICS grouping, nor with many other nations. China, with its amazing economic growth, has been asked to contribute more and more to the IMF and WB, and while its voting share has been just slightly increased it is still far below what it should be now based on the size of its economy.

---

* It might have been somewhat surprising for those who believe the Cold War between the Soviet Union and its bloc (on the one hand) and the U.S. led bloc (on the other) is long over, and can never resume, to read in a recent editorial in the British ruling class magazine, the *Economist*, that "America's security umbrella allows European countries to feel safe from, for instance, the possibility of future Russian aggression while spending little on defence." [July 6, 2013, p. 12.]

In fact, as of June 2013 China has just 3.81% of the voting shares in the IMF as compared with 16.75% for the U.S. An agreement was reached in 2010 that China's share could be raised to 6.068% provided that the IMF rules regarding such changes are followed. That means that 85% of the voting shares have to agree to the change. This in turn means that the U.S. can by itself veto any such changes, and so far it has refused to vote for the expansion of China's voting power! Needless to say this has greatly annoyed China, which has already won the support of over 78% of the voting shares. And even if China's vote *was* raised to 6%, it would still be less than half of the size it should be (in relation to the U.S.).[51]

This sort of arrogance on the part of the U.S., and its refusal to loosen its rigid and undemocratic control of the IMF, World Bank and other international institutions, has made China (and a number of other countries, including the other BRICS countries) think that maybe some *new* international economic and political institutions need to be constructed as alternatives to the ones so tightly controlled by the U.S. and its closest imperialist allies.

One current idea along these lines is the plan for the BRICS countries to set up an international development bank as an alternative to the World Bank (and to some degree an alternative to the IMF as well).

The idea for such a BRICS Development Bank was actually first raised some years ago. But on March 27, 2013, the leaders of the BRICS countries held a summit meeting in Durban, South Africa, and formally agreed to establish it.[52] In providing for the funding of infrastructure projects around the world it will be competing with the World Bank. But it will also create a "contingent reserve arrangement" worth $100 billion to help member countries counteract future financial shocks.[53] This is the sort of thing that the IMF does. The plan is not for these BRICS countries to *withdraw* from the IMF and WB at this time, but just to start building an alternative to them.

However, it is not yet clear how successful this particular plan to set up a new BRICS Development Bank is going to be. It must be recalled that the setting up of the World Bank and IMF themselves could not have happened when it did if the very disastrous World War II had not just taken place, and if there had not been the Great Depression of the 1930s which many people (erroneously) expected might resume after the War if drastic measures were not taken to ward it off.* Indeed, the World Bank was initially developed to formally institutionalize in permanent form the Marshall Plan, and its extension as a global credit plan. It is not at all clear that a similar sense of desperation among the "outs" within the current world imperialist system exists yet to get them to overcome their own contentions, hatreds and jealousies and set up effective alternative institutions to the World Bank and IMF.

One of the problems is that China wants to dominate the new BRICS bank in much the same way that the U.S. dominates the IMF and World Bank. (It is in the deepest nature of any capitalist-imperialist power to do this if it is able to.) China figures that since it has by far the biggest and fastest growing economy among the BRICS alliance, and since it will likely have to provide the largest contribution in capital to fund the bank, that it should basically be in charge of it.† But the other BRICS countries are reluctant to set up a new institution in which their voice is scarcely listened to, just as is the case with the current world institutions. One observer put it this way:

* The reason that many people, including many Marxists (also Stalin), expected that the Great Depression of the 1930s might resume after the artificial boom of World War II is that they failed to grasp Marx's explanation for how capitalist overproduction crises are resolved. As Marx & Engels noted, even as early as the *Communist Manifesto,* such crises are resolved only through the destruction of excess capital or else through the opening up of extensive new markets. Since virtually the whole world was already opened to capitalism by the 20th century, the only way left to resolve a major overproduction crisis from that point on was through the massive destruction of productive capital. And World War II did just that, especially in Europe and Asia. The U.S. economy benefitted after the war by the capital destruction elsewhere (even though there was no war destruction at home); and because so much machinery and productive capacity wore out at home during the war; and because of the forced growth of savings during the war when consumers had nothing substantial to buy (e.g., cars and appliances).

† The initial plan for the BRICS Bank is that each of the 5 countries will put in equal amounts; the figure of $10 billion each has been mentioned. But China wants each country to put in a larger amount to begin with, and only China will likely be able to add the huge additional capital later that the Bank will almost inevitably need.

> "Ironically it may be the cleavages within the BRICS grouping that more accurately hint at the future of the global order: tensions between China and Brazil on trade, India on security, and Russia on status highlight the difficulty Beijing will have in staking its claim to global leadership."[54]

Still, the primary fault line that seems to be developing within the world imperialist system is between the U.S. and its close allies (on the one hand), and China, Russia, the other BRICS countries, and still other primarily less economically developed countries angry at the U.S. and its allies (on the other hand). Remember once again that we are talking at the present time about developing *economic* blocs and contention, not about *war* blocs and alliances.*

While there have been trade disputes between Brazil and China, for example, at the same meeting in which the BRICS bank was chartered those two countries signed an agreement "to do billions of dollars of trade in their local currencies, as the BRICS nations work to lessen their dependence on the U.S. dollar and euro."[55] That attempt by BRICS and other countries to move away from the dollar and euro is also an important early indication that a new imperialist bloc might be gradually forming.

---

* There is a tendency that some people have to discount any possibility of growing economic contentions within the world imperialist system, and to deny even the possibility that different economic blocs might arise within the current world system, on the grounds that the U.S. currently has unchallengeable military power and unshakable military alliances with most of the other powerful countries of the world. We see this tendency as a sort of a neo-Kautskyian view similar to his theory of "ultra-imperialism". First, it fails to take to heart the reality of uneven development in the world, and the genuineness of the rapid growth of Chinese economic power in particular, along with the U.S. economic decline and fragility. Second, it confuses the present situation of growing *economic* contention with the possible future development of *military* contention. Third, philosophically, it seems to reject the important dialectical law that "one divides into two".

At the present time China cannot construct much of a "war bloc" against the U.S., except possibly with Russia. But that is not the issue now; no major interimperialist war is imminent (fortunately!). But economic contention is nevertheless developing rapidly, and will inevitably do so even more strongly as China continues to rise and the world economic crisis continues to develop.

The competition and hostility between India and China, however, may be much more serious than the differences between Brazil and China or Russia and China, and might lead India to break with the nascent BRICS alliance sometime in the future.

Probably the best way to view the situation at the present time is that this BRICS Development Bank plan is a major symptom of growing unrest and discord *within* the world imperialist system and a serious sign of the internal strains within that system that might *eventually* lead to its splitting up into separate and competing blocs. For now, the BRICS bank is sort of a tentative early step in that direction.

There are clearly echoes of one of the mythologized versions of the old Bandung idea here, of the "Third World" uniting against the imperialist "Center". But the central flaw of that version of the Bandung idea is even more evident here: If the countries uniting are themselves imperialist, sub-imperialist, or hoping to become such, the result can at most be a competing capitalist-imperialist bloc, and not a truly anti-imperialist alliance devoted to promoting genuine national liberation struggles.

It is not inconceivable that the BRICS bank, or some successor to it, might eventually prove to be an important and powerful alternative to the World Bank and the IMF. If the funding and support for those existing institutions fails in a major way, because of the growing seriousness of the world overproduction crisis and the increasingly dire financial crises associated with it (and the consequent inability of the U.S., Europe and Japan to adequately fund them†), then an alternative BRICS bank funded primarily by a still rising China might play a very important role in splitting the world imperialist system into two competing blocs.

From a pole or trend *within* the current world imperialist system it is possible that an eventual alternative, largely *independent* imperialist system might once again arise. But if this happens it will probably

† There are already signs of the increasing reluctance or inability of the U.S. to adequately fund the IMF and the World Bank. "Only recently Congress childishly refused to honor an agreed-upon increase in America's financial commitment to the International Monetary Fund." [*Economist*, Feb. 22, 2014, p. 8.]

only happen over a prolonged period of deepening economic crisis in which the U.S. in particular suffers some very major financial damage (such as the real collapse of the dollar). There are many possible scenarios here, and it is difficult to be absolutely certain about how all this will play out.

In any case, if this or other plans by China and its BRICS partners start to prove successful, they will undoubtedly start to attract the participation and support of other countries, including perhaps other fairly important economies such as Indonesia, Thailand and Mexico. Countries such as Argentina and Turkey, which have newly developing economic difficulties, may also be looking for new economic partners.* Capitalists in countries like South Korea have already started thinking that it is likely that their economic future may be more closely tied to China than to the U.S. There is therefore the potential for the BRICS economic bloc, or something similar to it, to expand considerably.

The same processes which appear to be leading to a new opposition bloc (like BRICS) within the world imperialist system are at the same time leading to weaknesses and growing disgruntlement and developing cracks between the U.S. and its closest allies.

One recent report on Germany's foreign policy commented that "the new signals from Germany's elite amount to a big change. They are based on the perception that America cannot or will not be around, as it once was, to solve Europe's problems in the future. Since revelations of American spying on Germans began last summer—the latest discovery is that America tapped not only Mrs Merkel's phone but also Mr Schröder's since 2002—trust in the former protector has been damaged… More generally, the debate reflects a new self-confidence in Germany."[56] Part of this new self-confidence is the idea that

* Turkey, for example, appeared to be relatively stable several years ago, but now shows increasing signs of economic weakness and political instability. It has had difficulties with Israel and in Syria, some differences of opinion with the U.S., and even the agreement with the Worker's Party of Kurdistan (PKK) to end a long armed rebellion shows signs recently of breaking down. Since the European Union (which has very serious internal problems itself) has been giving the cold shoulder to Turkey, that country might well be attracted to any rising BRICS bloc.

the German army will need to be more active abroad in the future.[57]

As we've mentioned there are jealousies and disagreements within the emerging opposition bloc (such as between China and Russia), but at the same time there are also growing disagreements and contentions within the remaining U.S.-led bloc as well! Contradictions exist everywhere. But the key to a political analysis of any situation is to discover and focus on the most important (primary) contradiction first of all.

12. Given the growing troubles of the U.S. and the whole world imperialist system, isn't it also dangerous to exaggerate the growth of Chinese imperialist power?

We definitely don't wish to "exaggerate" the growth of China's economic, political and military power—just to recognize its true extent and significance. Thus we are *not at all suggesting* that China will someday (perhaps "very soon"!) replace the U.S. as the lone superpower, and become the one totally dominant imperialist country in the world!

True, the U.S. is declining in both economic and political power, while China is rising in both spheres. But this is *not* the same thing as saying that China is going to *replace* the U.S. in the current world setup!

For one thing this notion falsely assumes that the nature of the present world is one totally dominated by a *single* imperialist country, and that any fundamental change in the present situation (other than world revolution ending imperialism totally) would have to mean the replacement of that dominant superpower by a *different* single dominant superpower. In other words, this notion implicitly rejects the central view we have been arguing for—that there is a *world imperial-*

ist system, and *not* just a world basically under the thumb of a single imperialist superpower.

The actual situation is that there is a rising new imperialist power currently operating *within* that single world imperialist system, but whose strength might possibly eventually lead to a split (to one degree or another) within that system and the formation once again of two independent or semi-independent imperialist blocs, one led by the U.S., and the other led by China. It is still early in the process, but we can already begin to see the growing possibility.

While China is not about to "replace" the U.S. within the world imperialist system, there are nevertheless ever more serious economic and political contradictions developing between them.

In the *economic sphere* China is rising very fast, and will almost certainly soon replace the U.S. as the world's largest economy. But even so, the U.S. will remain one of the world's most important economies long into the future. Even if the U.S. is the center of an intractable new world depression (as some of us expect over the next decade or two), and suffers a horrendous financial crisis far worse than that of 2008–2009, the U.S. economy will still be one of the largest and most important in the world. (Just as was the case for the U.S., Britain, France, Germany and Japan during the Great Depression of the 1930s.)

Politically and militarily, the situation is much less dire for the U.S., at least in the short and medium time frames. On the one hand their problems are very serious and steadily mounting, but on the other hand they still possess much more strength than China for many more years.

However, the outcomes of the long U.S.-led imperialist wars in Iraq and Afghanistan should be especially noted. On the one hand the U.S. has largely prevailed militarily *so far!* But on the other hand it has failed miserably from a political perspective in its goal of setting up stable neocolonial client regimes which can maintain order and facilitate present and future exploitation by the U.S. and the other imperialist countries. Considering the several trillion dollars the U.S. has blown on these efforts this blatant failure is quite remarkable.

And particularly ironic, China now seems to be doing a better job in grabbing the oil in Iraq than the U.S. is! This is causing no end to consternation within the U.S. ruling class.*

From the point of view of being able to utterly destroy any other country in an interimperialist world war, the U.S. is as strong as ever. The problem in that regard remains that Russia, and now also China, possess this same ability with regard to the U.S.

This means that interimperialist military contention, if it arises, and if both sides are sufficiently rational (by no means a given!) will have to take the form of proxy wars and the like. And the U.S. is incomparably stronger than China in this regard at present and most likely at least for years ahead, though here too the long-term trend is running against the U.S. It is important to recognize not only the present situation, but also the dynamic changes underway.

In any case, however, the U.S. is virtually certain to remain very powerful politically and militarily for a decade or more, despite the fact that its power and authority in both spheres is in fact gradually

---

* Tim Arango and Clifford Krauss, "China is Reaping Biggest Benefits of Iraq Oil Boom", *New York Times,* June 2, 2013, online at: http://www.nytimes.com/2013/06/03/world/middleeast/china-reaps-biggest-benefits-of-iraq-oil-boom.html?pagewanted=all&_r=0 "'We lost out,' said Michael Makovsky, a former Defense Department official in the Bush administration who worked on Iraq oil policy. 'The Chinese had nothing to do with the war, but from an economic standpoint they are benefiting from it, and our Fifth Fleet and air forces are helping to assure their supply.'"

Sometimes the angst within the U.S. ruling class about this almost becomes comical! Iraq has once again become one of the world's top oil producers, but as of June 2013 was shipping half of its production—an average of 1.5 million barrels a day—to China, and with China about to obtain even more of it. One liberal commentator, Robert Scheer, even claimed that this proves that "imperialism doesn't pay"! After all, so the thinking goes, the U.S. spent more than $3 trillion and lost more than 4,000 soldiers in its war in Iraq to secure that oil for itself, and now China is getting much of the oil instead! That doesn't seem fair to the U.S. imperialists. But of course these commentators are thinking about the older form of imperialism where imperialist powers owned colonies and their wealth outright. That is no longer how things work when there is a world imperialist *system* where all imperialist powers have the ability to exploit the neocolonies—once they are "pacified" through imperialist wars. [For more of this sort of lamentation and griping by the U.S. imperialists, see: "Issue of the Week: China's big oil buy", *The Week* magazine, June 14, 2013, p. 38.]

ebbing.

What we foresee is not China *replacing* the U.S., but rather China more and more *contending* with the U.S., for now within the world imperialist system, and quite possibly later in the form of two more or less distinct imperialist blocs.

13. Thinking about the social-imperialist USSR and what it means for China's status today.

Here is a little argument, sort of in the form of a syllogism, which should make Maoists who still doubt that China is now an imperialist country think a bit.

Most Maoists accept that the Soviet Union in its final decades was, as Mao himself labeled it, a *social-imperialist country*. That is, it was "socialist" in name, but imperialist in fact.

When the USSR/Russia dropped the socialist signboard did it cease to be an imperialist country? Of course not! True, Russia after the collapse of the USSR was not in nearly as strong a position to lord it over its former internal colonies and external satellites. It was not at that time in a position to invade Czechoslovakia and Hungary the way it had done before. But it owned large numbers of factories, mines and other facilities (including military bases) in the former states of the Soviet Union; it still exploited those countries; and it still threw its weight around when it could. (And the degree to which it has been able to do this has once again been growing in recent years.) The term now used by the Russian ruling class for its continuing imperialist sphere of special influence is "the near abroad".

Now consider present-day capitalist China as compared to contemporary Russia. China has, if anything, more foreign investments and operations than Russia; a much larger volume of exported capital, which is increasing at a vastly faster pace than that of Russia; a military force which is comparable to that of Russia; and it is beginning to throw its weight around in the world to a degree that at least matches Russia.

So if Russia is an imperialist country, then clearly China is too.

Or in abbreviated syllogistic form:

- The Soviet Union (dominated by Russia) in its last decades was an imperialist country (though nominally "socialist").
- Russia remained, and became a less disguised, imperialist country after it dropped the socialist signboard.
- China has all the same relevant characteristics, mostly to a greater degree, than imperialist Russia has.
- Therefore, China is an imperialist country too. QED.

14. China's huge and rapidly growing exports of capital.

It is time to discuss China's growing exports of capital in more depth. Lenin listed "the growing importance of the export of capital" as one of his defining characteristics of capitalist-imperialism. So this is a very important topic to seriously investigate when considering whether or not China is an imperialist country.

Foreign Direct Investment (FDI) is the acquisition by corporations of one country (whether state-owned or "private") of real assets in another country, such as factories, mines, or businesses. These assets may be acquired by building new factories, etc., or by simply purchasing existing factories and companies. FDI does not include the purchase of foreign securities (e.g., stocks and bonds), unless this amounts to buying a major or controlling influence in the foreign company that issues these securities. (The usual guideline is that ownership of more than 10% of a foreign company is considered to be FDI.)[58]

Thus China's huge foreign exchange reserves invested overseas and outward foreign "portfolio investment" (i.e., in foreign corporate stocks and bonds, etc.), now amounting to well over $1.2 trillion dollars in U.S. Treasury Bonds alone,* along with similar investments in Europe and elsewhere (though on a smaller scale), is *not counted* as outward FDI. But it nevertheless *is* a form of the export of capital! (As Lenin pointed out in the case of France's massive loans to Tsarist Russia in the pre-revolutionary period, that was still an export of capital which he said could be termed "usury imperialism". See section 5 above.)

This means that China's actual export of capital is *vastly larger* than most commentators are assuming when they consider only outward FDI. In fact, at this time, *by far the largest part* of China's export of capital is in the form of investments in foreign securities (including U.S. Treasury bonds), rather than in the direct purchase of foreign companies. (The clear trend, however, is for a growing proportion of China's capital exports to be in the form of FDI rather than merely in things like foreign reserve investments and portfolio investments.)

It is often pointed out that the amount of inward FDI *into* China from foreign imperialist countries far surpasses outward FDI *from* China to other countries, and this fact is used to argue that China is "on balance" not an international imperialist exploiter, but rather still a country which is more the victim of foreign imperialist exploitation. There are several deep flaws in this argument.

* As of December 2013, China's holdings of U.S. Treasury Securities were $1,268.9 billion. See: http://www.treasury.gov/resource-center/data-chart-center/tic/Documents/mfh.txt In addition, companies in Hong Kong (which of course is now officially part of China) hold $158.8 billion in U.S. Treasury bonds. Further large holdings of U.S. Treasuries by Chinese companies or agencies are probably hidden in the category that U.S. statistics call "Caribbean Banking Centers" (i.e., the Cayman Islands, Bahamas, Bermuda, etc.), in order to avoid the payment of taxes. The $290.9 billion of U.S. treasuries these "banking centers" officially hold are actually owned by other major investors around the world, and especially in Hong Kong and China. Thus the actual total holdings by Chinese corporations and government entities of U.S. Treasury securities is now probably around $1.5 trillion.

For one thing, if country A exports some of its capital to country B and thus exploits the working class there, while country B exports some of its own excess capital to country A and thus exploits the workers there, then *both of them* are engaged in international imperialist exploitation—and not just the country whose exports of capital (or foreign profits obtained) are the larger of the two!

But the biggest flaw in that argument is that FDI is not the *only* form of exported capital, and thus not the only form of international imperialist exploitation. The *total* (cumulative) outward flow of capital from China greatly exceeds the total inflow if *all* forms of capital, including invested foreign reserves and portfolio investment, are considered. In other words there is in fact *a net export of capital from China* despite the huge and still growing foreign investment within China.

A concept used by bourgeois economists discussing all forms of international capital imports and exports, and adding in all foreign assets and subtracting all forms of foreign financial "obligations", is the International Investment Position (IIP) for a given country at a given time.

Figure 14.1: China's International Investment Position, 2004–2012[59]

USD billion, total stock, assets (+) and liabilities (-)

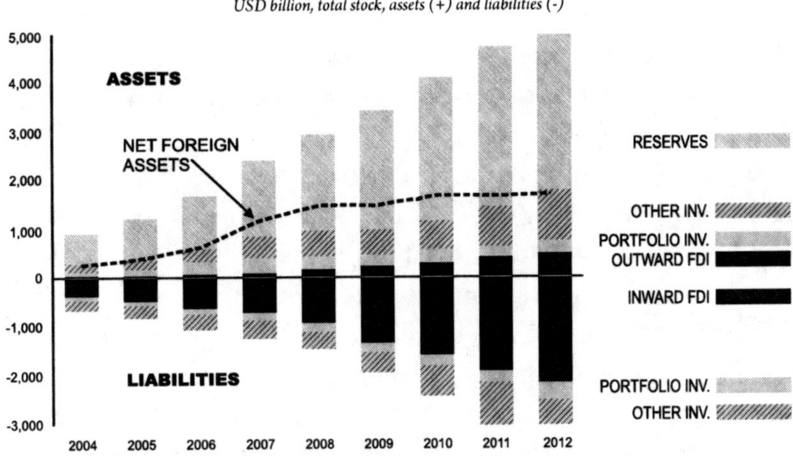

Source: PSOC, SAFE, RHG. * *Other investment category includes trade credit, loans, currency and deposits and other investment.*

As of the end of June in 2011, China's IIP stood at a colossal surplus of $2 trillion! Its external financial assets as of that date were $4.6 trillion, while its external financial liabilities at that time were $2.6 trillion. China's reserve assets, including gold, IMF Special Drawing Rights, reserve position in the IMF and foreign exchange reserves, totaled $3.3 trillion. (This amounted to 71% of China's total foreign financial assets at the time.) China's cumulative outward FDI at that date was $329.1 billion. Its outbound portfolio investment (in both corporate stocks and bonds) was $260.4 billion. Meanwhile inward FDI into China stood at $1.6 trillion. Thus, at the end of June 2011, China's actual total stock of capital exports stood at $4.6 trillion, and it even had a *net* International Investment Position of $2 trillion as of that time.[60]

Note that by subtracting the value of the inward FDI, inward portfolio investment, and other imports of capital into China, from China's outward FDI, invested reserves, portfolio investment, etc., the concept of "International Investment Position" itself vastly understates the levels of China's capital exports. True, its *net* export of capital was "just" $2 trillion at the end of June 2011, but its *actual level* of capital exports still totaled $4.6 trillion as of that date. The fact that the U.S. and other countries send their own excess capital to China, for example, does not actually diminish in any way the amount of capital that China exports to other countries. The fact that foreign countries exploit Chinese workers by sending capital to China in no way diminishes China's own exploitation of foreign workers when it exports capital to other countries!

We should keep this difference between the actual level of capital exports, and the abstract bookkeeping balance known as "IIP", in mind as we look at Figure 14.1 above, which shows China's international investment position for the years 2004–2012.

Note first that China's "net foreign assets" have been positive and quite substantial for this entire period, and have exceeded $1 trillion since 2007 and $2 trillion since mid-2011. Note also that China's level of "net foreign assets" has continued to grow over this period, though its rate of growth has considerably slowed down during the last 5 years (the period of the "Great Recession" in the world). Note that the moving of capital into China and the export of capital out of China both continue to expand at a fast pace. And note especially that China's total cumulative export of capital reached around $5 trillion at the end of 2012.

How does this compare to the United States? First of all, the U.S. net international investment position at the end of the first quarter of 2013 was a *negative* $4.277 trillion![61] (As compared to a *positive* $2 trillion for China.) What's more, this U.S. IIP figure is over $400 billion worse than just 3 months earlier! So from an IIP standpoint, China is far ahead of the U.S. (and in far better financial shape generally). It is also worth noting that according to *Forbes* (the U.S. business magazine) about 7.5% of U.S. government debt is now owned by China.[62]

However, we need to stress once again that the net IIP value is *not* the proper way to determine the level of *exported capital* for any country, whether that be the U.S. or China. Despite its very negative IIP, the U.S. still has a cumulative pile of exported capital totaling $21.618 trillion. However, foreign-owned assets in the U.S. totaled $25.896 trillion, which leads to the net negative balance of over $4 trillion in the IIP.[63]

China's total exported capital, at around $5 trillion in 2012, is therefore still only about ¼ of that of the U.S. But it is nevertheless enormous, growing rapidly, and already in the same range as (or bigger than!) that of many other imperialist countries.[64]

Like China, much of the U.S. assets overseas are also not in the form of FDI. According to OECD figures only $5 trillion of U.S. overseas assets were in the form of FDI as of 2012.[65]

While outward FDI is only a small portion of total exported capital, it is nevertheless of particular importance and interest. So we'll now investigate China's outward FDI in more detail.

15. China's outward Foreign Direct Investment (FDI).

As of the end of 2012, China's accumulated stock of outward FDI was $502.8 billion.[66]

Although China's accumulated total of outward FDI (i.e., its OFDI *stock*) is still small compared with many other imperialist countries, it is larger than that of Russia and is growing at a faster rate than that of all other imperialist or sub-imperialist countries.

China is still way behind most of the other imperialist countries in *total* "stock" of outward FDI for the simple reason that it got a much later start in accumulating these foreign assets. But its rate of growth of such assets—at more than twice the rate of growth of U.S. outward FDI stocks—is now very rapidly closing the gap.

How very recent the accumulation of a significant amount of outward FDI has been for China can be seen in Figure 15.2. China began to export capital in a very tiny way in the 1980s. This small outflow picked up just a bit in the 1990s, but it wasn't until the new century that it really began to jump up in a major way. At first the target destinations were mostly in Southeast Asia. And from the start most of the outward FDI was being done by Chinese state-owned enterprises (SOEs).* One notable exception was the acquisition of IBM's personal computer unit by the then private Lenovo Corporation in 2005.† In mid-2013 Lenovo became the largest computer company in the world.[68]

Starting around 2005 China's export flow of capital in the form of outward foreign direct investment took a qualitative leap upward,

---

* Officially China's private corporations accounted for only 9.5% of China's total outward FDI in 2012, though that was up from less than 4% in the two previous years. [*Economist*, "China's overseas investment", Jan. 19, 2013.] However, there is reason to believe that the amount of Chinese private investment overseas is being greatly understated by the Chinese government, as we will discuss in the section on Chinese investment in Africa.

† The Chinese Academy of Science, a state agency, later bought 28.6% of Lenovo in July 2009.

Figure 15.1: Comparing China's Outward FDI "Stock" to that of Other Countries [In billions of U.S. dollars][67]

	TOTAL OFDI STOCK (2011) *(a)*	NEW OFDI FLOW IN 2012 *(b)*	TOTAL OFDI STOCK (2012) *(c)*	% INCREASE IN STOCK IN 2012 *(d)*
BRAZIL	206.2	- 2.8	270.9 (?)	?
CHINA	424.8	62.4	502.8	18.4
FRANCE	1,478.6	37.2	1,540.1	4.2
GERMANY	1,423.2	67.0	1,539.8	8.2
INDIA	109.5	8.6	118.2	7.9
ITALY	519.7	29.8	535.0	2.9
JAPAN	955.9	122.5	1,037.7	8.6
RUSSIA	361.5	28.4	387.2	7.1
S. AFRICA	97.1	3.0	111.8	15.1
U.K.	1,696.2	77.7	1,793.2	5.7
U.S.	4,663.1	388.3	5,077.8	8.9

Total OFDI stock means the current value of all outward FDI flows up through the end of the year mentioned. The OECD figure for Brazil in 2012 seems quite inconsistent with the fact that Brazil had negative "outflows" of OFDI in both 2011 and 2012. (However, for all the countries the total stock amount for 2012 is not a simple addition of the 2011 total with the new flow in 2012, because the existing stock can also change in value, such as through inflation.) The percentage increase in column (d) is derived by: [column (c) – column (a)] / column (a).

Figure 15.2 China's Early Outward Foreign Direct Investment (Yearly figures in US$ billions, 1979–2006)[69]

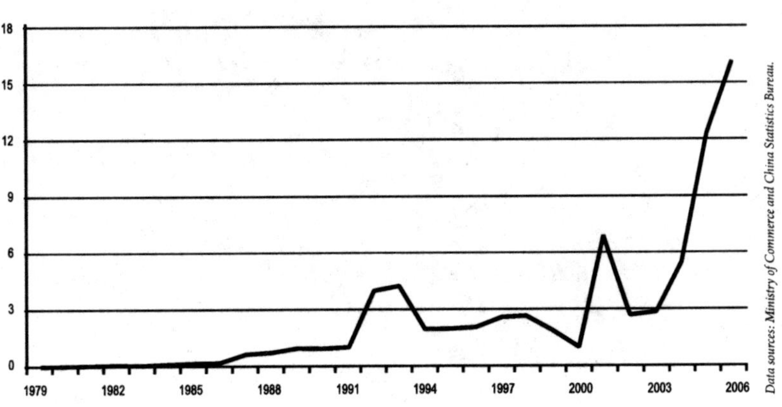

and since then it has been growing enormously, reaching, as we mentioned, $62.4 billion in 2012 alone.

China's outward FDI is being sent to all parts of the world. The top four countries in recent years have been Australia, the U.S., Canada and Brazil (see chart below).[70]

In Australia Chinese investments were first especially heavy in mining, focusing in particular on iron ore, and in oil, gas and other natural resources. More recently in Australia, however, China has been diversifying and investing in food, agribusiness, real estate, renewable energy industries, high tech and financial services.[71]

While the graph below shows Canada in 3rd place as a target for China's outward FDI for the whole 2005–12 period, for just the single year of 2012 Canada was the largest single target country. The Chinese oil giant CNOOC purchased Nexen, Inc., for $15 billion, and other Chinese investments in 2012 brought the total FDI flow into Canada that year to $23 billion.[72]

As that one mammoth investment suggests, China's FDI in Canada has mostly been in oil & gas, and mining. (China has been a major importer of nickel, copper, iron ore and potash from Canada.) While

China's Biggest Outward FDI Targets

2005–12 $bn

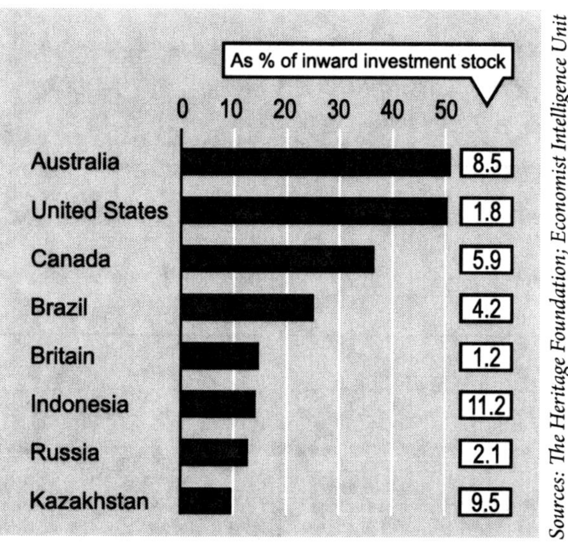

China's investments in many countries (including Australia and the U.S.) have begun a major trend toward diversification, in Canada it is natural resources which remain the primary target.

In Brazil Chinese FDI investment was also primarily focused on the energy and metals industries through 2010. In 2011, however, only about 20% of the new FDI flow from China was in mining, with another 20% in agribusiness, and about 50% in the technology sector. China has begun making some major investments in Brazilian manufacturing and infrastructure areas, such as electricity production and distribution, a trend which China's ambassador to Brazil recently indicated would be stepped up.[73]

China has been Brazil's biggest trading partner since 2009. According to one source, from 1990 to 2009 Brazil represented 3.5% of China's outward FDI, but this has really jumped up since then.[74] The stock of China's FDI in Brazil before 2009 was only around $200 million, but increased to more than $21 billion in the 2009–2012 period.[75]

A world map showing the locations of China's largest overseas investments since 2005 (i.e., those worth at least $100 million each), including some attempted acquisitions that have been blocked by the U.S. or other governments, is the Heritage Foundation's China Global Investment Tracker Interactive Map at: http://www.heritage.org/research/projects/china-global-investment-tracker-interactive-map (The deep concern shown about China's global expansion by reactionary ruling class think tanks such as the Heritage Foundation reflects the tremendous fears of the U.S. bourgeoisie with regard to China's rise.)

What about China's Foreign Direct Investments in the U.S.? Chinese FDI is going to all parts of the country, with the top five states so far being California, New York, Texas, Illinois and North Carolina. North Carolina has gotten continued special attention in part because of the large 2005 purchase by Lenovo of IBM's personal computer business which is headquartered there (which encouraged other Chinese companies to also invest in the state), and because of special efforts by N.C. state authorities to lure more Chinese companies.[76]

Estimates of the stock (total amount) of Chinese FDI in the U.S. as of the end of 2012 vary from $23 billion to $50 billion, but the higher figure may include some investment which should actually be termed portfolio investment.[77]

Chinese direct investment in the U.S. would be much higher if the U.S. government had not blocked some major deals (supposedly for "security" reasons), and if Chinese companies had not come to view the U.S. as being a somewhat "difficult environment" to invest in, in part because of anti-Chinese attitudes here. "Many Chinese firms recall the uproar that sank the 2005 rejection of China National Offshore Oil Corp's $18.5 billion attempt to buy U.S. energy company Unocal. That chilled Chinese investment in the United States for two years."[78]

However, more recently China's direct investment in the U.S. has nevertheless picked up considerably. Through May there was $10.5 billion in new direct investments in the U.S. in 2013. The planned purchase by Shuanghui International Holdings of the Smithfield Foods, the world's largest hog producer, for nearly $5 billion will be the largest single Chinese acquisition in the U.S. so far, if it goes ahead. (There have been a few pious Congressional fears expressed about "the safety of the food supply", but the deal is expected to go through.)[79]

Besides the large Smithfield and original Lenovo deals, some other major Chinese direct investments in the U.S. include the purchase of AMC Entertainment (the movie theater chain) for $2.6 billion in 2012; the purchase of the Volvo division from Ford by the Zhejian Geely Holding Group in 2010 for a total of $1.5 billion; the recent purchase of the bankrupt ion battery maker A123 by the Wanxiang Group for $256.5 million (which had Congressmen grumbling because the U.S. government had previously given the company $249 million in Recovery Act money to try to keep it going); the takeover of MiaSole, a California solar panel maker, by Hanergy Group, China's largest privately owned renewable energy company, for a mere "tenth of its asking price in the midst of a downturn in the market"; Sinopec's (China's second-largest energy company) purchase of 1/3 of Devon Energy's Oklahoma oil projects in 2012; the 2013 Sinopec purchase of 1/3 of the Chesapeake Energy Corp. for $2.2 bil-

Laos is the victim of massive deforestation by Chinese and Vietnamese logging companies, which is also causing serious soil erosion and forcing large numbers of people off the land.[92]

This railroad will generate huge wealth for China, much more so than for Laos. It is important to China not only for expanding the exploitation of Laos, but actually for hugely expanding its operations in Southeast Asia more generally. The rail line will connect with the existing railroad from Vientiane to Bangkok—a very important center of trade—and then be extended to Dawei (and thus to Rangoon) in the Bay of Bengal in Myanmar.[93] This will provide a land route which bypasses the Malacca Straits, a potential choke point between China's east coast and the Indian Ocean.

As for Laos itself, China has been granted authority by the Laotian government to operate a number of Special Economic Zones there. China has so many projects underway in the country (including building construction in Vientiane, and even the construction of a large "Chinatown" for over 100,000 Chinese people), that "Some Laotians, unhappy with the unmistakable Chinese presence, complain that their country is becoming little more than a province of China or, more slyly, a vassal state."[94]

In Nepal Chinese investment so far is less rapacious. One reason is that China is in effect bribing Nepal with development projects in order to secure complete cooperation by Nepal's government in suppressing any Tibetan refugee and independence movements operating there. (This is one of many examples of how Chinese political pressure is already being used in other countries.)

China is also planning to build a railroad from Tibet to Kathmandu in Nepal. The Lhasa–Shigatse railway is currently under construction and should be finished in 2014. China has told Nepal that as soon as that link is finished it will start on the Shigatse–Kathmandu segment.[95]

However, even before that rail link is started, China has already displaced India as the largest source of FDI coming into Nepal.[96] But India is still the largest trade partner with Nepal, and that may continue even after the completion of the China–Nepal railroad (because of the vast distances through Tibet and western China to the major Chinese industrial areas).

Neverthless, China's activity and influence in Nepal has been rapidly increasing. China has been deepening its military ties with Nepal by providing weapons, other supplies and training to the reactionary Nepal Army.[97]

China's FDI in Latin America has also been growing very rapidly, and not just in Brazil which we discussed earlier. One study in 2012 starts by stating that "Chinese investment in Latin America has exploded in recent years." This study, which focused on Chinese mining investment in Peru, found that the negative impacts of Chinese companies operating there have not been "significantly worse" than that of other foreign or local capitalist corporations from the point of view of their economic, environmental and social impact.[98] (But what a ridiculous standard that is! It is like "defending" the Chicago Mafia gangsters as being "no worse" than the mob in New York!)

Trade between China and Latin America reached $261.2 billion in 2012.[99] That is just as much as Chinese trade with Africa, which gets more international attention. And Chinese investment to Latin America (including Brazil) *exceeds* its investment in Africa. Moreover, development loans from the China Development Bank and the Export-Import Bank of China since 2005 have actually exceeded that provided by the World Bank or the Inter-American Development Bank during that period.[100] China, *by itself,* and before the BRICS

Development Bank even gets functioning in a significant way, is already more important for economic development in many parts of the world than is the World Bank! The sort of development underway, of course, is that which is in line with China's own imperialist economic interests and profits.

Chinese companies are building many energy and infrastructure projects in Latin America, including a $4.7 billion project by China's Gezhouba Corporation of building two new hydroelectric facilities in Santa Cruz, Argentina. Similarly the Chinese company SinoHydro is building a $2.2 billion hydroelectric project in Ecuador.[101]

Of course, much of Chinese investment in Latin America is for the purpose of acquiring bulk commodities and natural resources, such as Peru's copper, Brazil's iron ore, and Argentina's soya crops. In recent years more that 64% of Chinese OFDI in Latin America has been focused on raw materials and commodities, though more diversification may now be occurring.[102]

China's SOEs are responsible for as much as 87% of Chinese OFDI in Latin America, according to a study by Tufts University,[103] though it is very likely that this percentage is now falling from year to year as private Chinese corporations begin to export more and more capital.

16. China's "Go Global" Strategy.

What accounts for such a rapid expansion of China's outward FDI in recent years? To a large degree it has been the result of a conscious policy on the part of the Chinese ruling class, known as the "Go Global" strategy. First some background information.

Ken Davies, a consultant for the OECD Investment Division, notes in his important 2013 study, "China Investment Policy: An Update", that "China has been rapidly becoming an important source of outward foreign direct investment (OFDI), a trend that was reinforced by the global financial and economic crisis."[104] This point about the role of the global crisis in reinforcing this outward FDI from China is worth thinking about for a moment.

It is sometimes argued that Chinese capitalism is so dependent upon exporting *commodities* to foreign countries that the rapid growth of the Chinese economy in recent decades is bound to soon come to a screeching halt as the world economy sinks deeper into crisis and stops expanding its huge purchases of so many goods from China. There are serious problems with this thesis.

First, even if the world economy is in crisis and slows down in a major way (as it has already done), or even seriously contracts in a prolonged and ever-deepening way (as it is likely to do in coming years), there is still the possibility of *some* countries doing much better than others. And those that are likely to do best under these more adverse general conditions are those like China with still lots of relatively poorly paid but productive workers, an ever improving infrastructure, and a more stable financial situation.

A world economic crisis intensifies international competition, and a country like China that has been *winning* this competition will suffer far less from the crisis than other countries. (At least in its early periods, and if political stability can be maintained there by the ruling class.)*

---

* Of course in saying that "China is likely to suffer far less" in the early periods of this world crisis we are still talking about the situation from the point of view of the ruling class. That is, we are talking about the measurement of pain in the terms the capitalists use—as harm to GDP, worsening trade balances, etc., and not primarily how the masses are affected. Of course all capitalist economic crises always fall hardest on the backs of the working classes, and that goes for every country including China.

How stable is China politically? This is not completely clear. On the one hand the rapid growth of the economy has led to the creation of a quite large "middle class" (mostly consisting of the highest paid urban workers, rather than merely a petty bourgeoisie properly speaking). On the other hand there are hundreds of millions of downtrodden peasants, many migrating to the cities, and other workers at the lower levels of society who—if they can find work at all—are very low paid and horribly treated. And there are at least tens of thousands of serious mass protests, of one kind or another, in China every year. Despite such widespread rebellion among those sectors of the population which could not be

Second, this thesis ignores the major and intensifying campaign by the Chinese ruling class to refocus its economy *away from being export-oriented,* and more towards promoting its internal growth, though in a manner further integrated within the globalized production system.[105]

Third, the thesis that China, as an export-oriented country, will especially suffer as the world economic crisis intensifies seems to forget that modern capitalist-imperialist countries have an important supplement or alternative to the export of commodities, namely *the export of capital!* The primary reason that the export of capital became so important in the imperialist era is that the home markets in the leading capitalist countries became satiated and there was a growing scarcity of profitable investment opportunities there. This is mostly what leads imperialist countries to export so much capital in the first place!

Actually, it is not at all clear that the home market in China *is* completely satiated, though there is certainly at least temporary overproduction in many sectors. Of course, if we understand how capitalism is based on the generation of surplus value we also understand that no capitalist market can expand, and continue to expand, unless there is also the continuous expansion of consumer and/or government debt to enable it. But it appears that the level of both consumer and government debt in China is still much lower than in the U.S., Europe or Japan. There is a lot of *local government debt* in China, but the more important national government debt is much less of a worry so far.[106] As the *Economist* magazine recently stated, "China's government as a whole is able to sustain its debts without undue strain on the economy."[107] Plus the tighter government control of the banks and financial sphere in China also gives them much more scope for the further expansion of debt (without an early financial collapse)—and thus the possibility of prolonging the boom economy there is much

---

fully integrated into this new capitalist economy, China has had a relatively stable economic advance over recent decades. But there are too many contradictory factors to be sure if this relative stability will continue for a long time yet into the future.

greater than elsewhere.* However, this doesn't mean that there can't be economic slowdowns in China too and maybe even some outright recessions at times.†

In any case, even before the U.S. and world financial crisis of 2008–9 broke out, China began reorienting its whole economy away from the simple export of cheap commodities, and more in the direction of globalization and the export of capital. And since the "Great Recession" began, this reorientation has intensified. As we mentioned earlier in this essay, exports of goods fell from 38% of Chinese GDP in 2007 to just 26% in 2012.[108] Some Western specialists in the Chinese economy say that the internal consumption of goods within China is even substantially higher than official statistics show because of the large size of the "underground economy".[109]

Thus, somewhat ironically, the need to refocus the Chinese economy partially *away from* the export of cheap commodities and much more toward the export of capital is the essence of the major nationwide economic campaign in China to "Go Outward" or "Go Global!"

Before the year 2000 the Chinese government carefully limited outward direct investment by both private and state-owned enterprises (SOEs). But this policy was diametrically changed with the "Go Global" policy (*zou-chu-qu,* literally "go out") announced by Premier Zhu Rongji in 2000 in his report to the National People's Congress. Though now a capitalist country, China still has "Five Year Plans" to give general guidance to the development of its economy. The Tenth Five-Year Plan (2001–05) made overseas investment by Chinese enterprises one of the four key thrusts designed to adjust the Chinese economy to the reality of economic globalization within the world capitalist system. In March 2004 Premier Wen Jiabao urged

* Because the Chinese government already owns, controls and directs the largest banks, when there is a financial crisis the government does not need to go through the complicated and politically contentious step of first nationalizing the failing financial institutions. It can instead proceed directly to the step of either propping up the banks by creating and giving them money, or else apportioning the necessary debt write-offs as it deems appropriate.

† Even within overall boom periods, such as the quarter century in the U.S. after World War II, there can still be recessions. There were several fairly short mild or moderate recessions in the U.S. during this overall boom period.

that the implementation of this "Go Global" policy should be sped up and that the government should coordinate and guide Chinese investment abroad more effectively. Enterprises under all forms of ownership were strongly encouraged to invest in overseas operations and expand their international market shares. And this "Go Global" strategy was stressed again in the Eleventh Five-Year Plan (2006–10).[110]

But with the intensification of the global economic crisis in 2008 this "Go Global" strategy was further elaborated, promoted and greatly sped up even more. Chinese outward FDI flows more than doubled from 2007 to 2008 "when Chinese investors found themselves in a privileged financial position and could take advantage of the crisis then hitting their competitors in more developed countries."[111] And Wen Jiabao, in presenting the outline of the current (Twelfth) Five-Year Plan in October 2010 again stated that "We must accelerate the implementation of the 'go global' strategy".[112] On March 15, 2011 Premier Wen elaborated further:

> "We will accelerate the implementation of the 'go global' strategy, improve relevant support policies, simplify examination and approval procedures, and provide assistance for qualified enterprises and individuals to invest overseas. We will encourage enterprises to operate internationally in an active yet orderly manner. We will strengthen macro guidance over overseas investments, improve the mechanisms for stimulating and protecting them, and guard against investment risks."[113]

Note especially the comment here about the Chinese government "protecting" and "guarding" overseas investments! This is a primary role of any imperialist military machine.

And this "Go Global" strategy is not just abstract talk or hopeful dreams. Serious pressure is being put on Chinese companies (SOEs or otherwise), and all the regions of China, to actively participate in this strategy. Chinese businessmen operating overseas often mention this intensifying pressure at home to "Go Global".

Partly by coincidence, and partly by design, as the growth rates in the exports of Chinese made goods slow down, the growth rates for the export of Chinese FDI and other forms of capital are being greatly increased.

We noted in section 14 above that although China's inward FDI from other countries presently far exceeds its outward FDI to foreign countries, nevertheless China's *total export of capital* still exceeds the total imports of capital by at least $2 trillion. Still, the specific imbalance between inward and outward FDI bothers the Chinese rulers and one of the major goals of the Twelfth Five-Year Plan is to more closely balance these investment flows. The Chinese Minister of Commerce, Chen Deming, stated on March 7, 2011, that in 2010 the ratio of outward FDI to inward FDI was 6 to 10, but that the plan is to bring this ratio into balance (1 to 1) within 5 to 10 years.[114]

A couple months later, Zheng Chao, a senior Ministry of Commerce official in the Department of Outward Investment and Economic Cooperation, said that outward FDI would grow annually by "20 to 30 percent" over the next five years, and that outward FDI would overtake inward FDI "within three years" (rather than the previously estimated five or more years).[115] That new timetable may not yet be a certainty, but what *is* certain is that China is taking major steps to soon bring inward and outward FDI flows into a balance.

The Chinese bourgeoisie is also worried about mass unrest, and the large number of "mass incidents" in recent years.* This is part of the reason why they are allowing workers' wages to rise. But rising wages (and perhaps benefits) will also serve to make China a somewhat less favorable location for foreign direct investment. However, as we mentioned in an endnote earlier (page 22), China surpassed the U.S. for the first time in 2012 as the favorite country in the world for inward foreign direct investment. And even with rising wages, it is likely to remain a favorite target for foreign investment for years to come—especially considering the persistent economic problems in the U.S., Europe and Japan.

This means that if the difference between inward and outward FDI is to find a better balance, it must of necessity mostly come about—

* There have been over 100,000 such "mass incidents" annually in recent years (by official Chinese government reports!), such as wildcat strikes, farmers protesting the theft of their land for industrial projects and real estate development, protests against corruption and protests against various environmental outrages.

for the time being at least—through greatly expanded outward FDI from China. This is yet another reason to expect that China's outward FDI, in accordance with its "Go Global" strategy, will continue to rapidly expand for a long time.[116]

There are many motives behind China's "Go Global" strategy, and some of the motives may not be initially obvious. For example, a top priority in this campaign is the creation and promotion of a large number of "global champions", i.e., large Chinese based multinational corporations with globally recognized brands able to better compete in the international market.[117] One of the problems for Chinese capitalist-imperialism has been the difficulty of establishing recognized and respected brand names for Chinese commodities, and this is one of the specific problems that the "Go Global" strategy is designed to overcome.†

Of course another major motive behind the "Go Global" strategy is just to more easily acquire foreign technology and know-how. Some studies have shown (as one might expect) that it is much easier to acquire foreign technology through outward FDI investment than it is from inward investment by foreign corporations.[118] And setting up companies or branches of companies overseas also allows an end-run around the still considerable international barriers to trade (including import quotas, tariffs, and other obstacles).[119]

But beyond such important goals as these, the *primary reason* for the "Go Global" strategy is the basic necessity to export capital which all capitalist-imperialist countries share: the need to find and exploit the most profitable places around the world for the investment of excess capital.

---

† It is simply not true, as some people have maintained, that it is impossible to outflank the U.S. and other established imperialist countries because of their well-known and supposedly impregnable brand names. For more general information about the techniques that not only China, but also other countries relatively new to the world market are using to build or acquire prominent and recognizable brand names, see: "The emerging-brand battle: Western brands are coming under siege from developing-country ones", *Economist*, June 22, 2013, p. 70. One example from that article: "Pearl River of China has become the world's biggest piano-maker and now rivals Yamaha (itself once an emerging-market challenger) on quality."

17. China's special focus on Africa.

China has been making a special focus on Africa, and this has drawn a lot of attention not only in Africa itself, but in the U.S., Europe and Japan. It worries the other imperialist powers that China is making such headway in the exploitation of a continent which they haven't paid much attention to themselves.* If you use Google to search for "China's investments in Africa" you will find literally thousands of recent articles on the topic, and enormous numbers of briefer references.

One surprising thing is that not that large a fraction of China's huge and rapidly expanding foreign investment is actually going to Africa![120] According to China's official reckoning, only 2.2% of "outward foreign direct investment" (OFDI) from China, including both private and state-led investment, currently goes to Africa.[121]

However, several things must be kept in mind here. First, even just 2.2% of a vast amount is still a pretty large sum. Second, Africa has been so undeveloped for so long a time that even relatively small amounts of investment can have a huge impact. Investing the equivalent of tens or hundreds of millions of dollars in an African country can have a larger impact than investing billions might in major European countries. Seven of the fastest growing (though still quite

---

* "Africa, a continent that has been neglected by Americans, has been targeted by China as a land of opportunity because of its rich reserves of oil, iron ore, copper, gold, and other minerals." —Susan L. Shirk, *China: Fragile Superpower* (Oxford Univ. Press, 2007), p. 134. [Shirk is a former Deputy Assistant Secretary of State responsible for U.S. relations with China.]

More recently, White House deputy national security advisor Ben Rhodes had this to say: "What we hear from our businesses is that they want to get in the game in Africa. There are other countries getting in the game in Africa—China, Brazil, Turkey. And if the U.S. is not leading in Africa, we're going to fall behind in a very important region of the world." Quoted in Patrick Bond, "Obama in South Africa: Washington tells Pretoria how to 'play the game' in Africa", June 30, 2013, posted on Frontlines of Revolutionary Struggle, at http://revolutionaryfrontlines.wordpress.com/2013/06/08/washington-in-africa-who-will-obama-whack-next/#more-26581

small) economies in the world at present are in Africa, and Chinese FDI there is a major reason for this.[122]

And third, China is considerably underreporting its levels of foreign investment, *especially in Africa*. It appears to be doing this because the Chinese penetration into Africa has become such a touchy subject. (See Figure 17.1 below.)

In April 2013 the *Financial Times* in London published information which showed even more clearly that not only the number of Chinese projects in Africa is being grossly understated, but so is the dollar amounts of the FDI involved. Their study showed that a majority of the Chinese projects in Africa, and a rapidly expanding majority of the value involved in them, are "unofficial" (which presumably means they are being done by private Chinese corporations) and hence are not included in official Chinese government statistics about the outward FDI to Africa.[123]

China, in the Maoist era, had a long record of *genuinely* supporting economic development in Africa, and made a lot of friends there. There were some famous infrastructure projects built by China in Africa for the benefit of the people there, such as the major Tanzania–Zambia railroad project.† After capitalism was restored in China, the new ruling bourgeoisie, as is typical of that class, sought to "capitalize" on the good feelings that had developed in Africa toward China during the socialist era.

---

† The Tazara Railway (also known as the Uhuru Railway or Tanzam Railway) links the port of Dar es Salaam in Tanzania with the town of Kapiri Mposhi in Zambia's Central Province. This massive $500 million project was completely financed and built by China in its Maoist revolutionary years as a gift to landlocked Zambia, to lessen its economic dependence on the white-minority colonial governments of Rhodesia (now Zimbabwe) and South Africa. (China also intended to open up crucial military supply lines to liberation movements in southern Africa, including the Pan-African Congress of Azania, FRELIMO in Mozambique and ZANU in Zimbabwe.) Construction began in 1970 and was completed in 1975, two years ahead of schedule. However, in later decades, when revolutionary solidarity no longer characterized capitalist China's relationship to neocolonial Africa, the railroad has been allowed to fall into considerable disrepair, and it no longer has the great economic importance that it once did. Some information here is from the Wikipedia at: https://en.wikipedia.org/wiki/TAZARA_Railway

Figure 17.1:
Number of Chinese Investments in 6 African Countries
(as reported by China and by the Host countries themselves)[124]

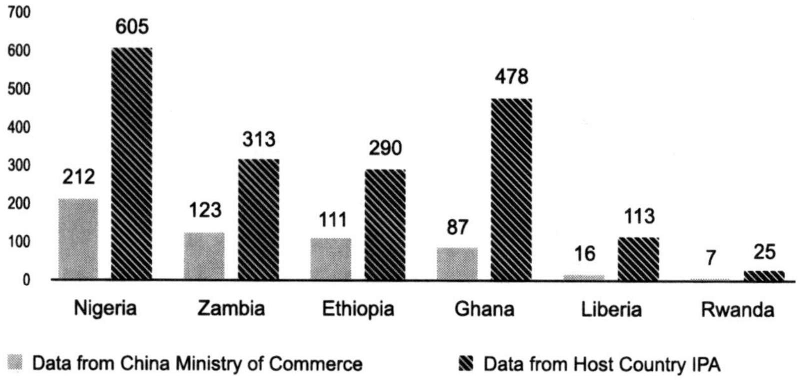

Data as of the end of 2011.

And China, even as the capitalist-imperialist country it is today, has mounted a significant media operation to portray its investments in Africa as being for the purpose of benefiting the people there. Moreover, China has paid much more attention to presenting the appearance of equality and friendship toward African regimes, rather than the typical arrogance of the U.S. and most European imperialist countries. China has the advantage of not having had a history of imperialist conquest and colonial rule in Africa (as is the case with Britain, France, Portugal, Belgium, Italy, etc.), and—so far—of having had only limited military interference in Africa.* And finally, China has not deigned to denounce undemocratic regimes in

* However, China has already sent naval ships to the area off the coast of East Africa to combat Somali and other pirates. China also has military attachés in 14 African countries, and in 2004 dispatched about 1,500 soldiers in Liberia and the Democratic Republic of the Congo which operated under the auspices of the U.N. ["China's trade safari in Africa". *Le Monde Diplomatique,* May 11, 2005.] These have been the very eager (if still early and limited) attempts by China to demonstrate that it can also throw its military weight around. We will further discuss China's military activity in Africa in the section of the essay on the Chinese military.

Africa and elsewhere (partly no doubt because it does not even have bourgeois democratic institutions itself!), nor to complain about the common violations of human rights in Africa (except in a few cases where these have fallen on Chinese citizens). As one South African businessman put it, China is the first big foreign power to come to Africa without acting "as though they are some kind of patron or teacher or conqueror."[125]

All this is used, not only by China, but also by many foreign observers who are rather easily fooled by such surface decorations, to portray the present Chinese capitalist economic penetration into Africa in a prettier light, and even to suggest that it is something qualitatively "different" than imperialism. It is sometimes claimed that China refuses to engage in the same "arrogant imperialist economic domination" of Africa as other countries have done in the past, or that it is some sort of "softer power". And it is even claimed that China's actual rapidly growing economic domination in many parts of Africa does not reflect any hegemonic ambitions on the part of China. (If economic penetration and developing economic domination does not mean establishing hegemony, then *what does it mean?!*)

The argument seems to be that robbery is not really robbery if one of your cohorts (the U.S., Britain or France, at present, or else some local politician in your pay) is actually holding the gun for you while you help yourself to the victim's valuables; that robbery is not really robbery if it is done without as many gratuitous arrogant threats and insults as robbers typically spread about; that robbery is not really robbery if you are slightly more generous to your inside partners (local politicians) in the country you are looting; and that robbery is not really robbery if you are new to the business and your father and grandfather were not also robbers! We find this sort of apologetics for rapidly rising Chinese imperialist economic robbery in Africa, and elsewhere, quite deceptive and disingenuous!

South African President Jacob Zuma recently gave this advice to the old-line imperialists: "I've said it to the private sector from the western countries, 'Look, you have got to change the way you do business with Africa if you want to regain Africa. If you want to treat Africa as a former colony, then people will go to new partners.'"[126]

Of course China is especially the sort of "new partner" Zuma had in mind.

And it is true that China has a more effective way of "doing business" in Africa than the older imperialist powers. But this in no way means that China is itself not an imperialist country exploiting Africa; rather, it only means that China is a smarter, less arrogant "partner" to the local comprador ruling classes in African countries, and thus the foreign capitalist-imperialist country that is now *outcompeting* with the other imperialist countries in the new contest for Africa.

Trade between Africa and China increased by 700% during the 1990s,[127] and since 2010 China has been Africa's largest trading partner.[128] It was estimated in August 2007 that there were more than 750,000 Chinese nationals working in various African countries,[129] and by 2013 more than one million Chinese citizens were residing in Africa.[130] (That's in addition to a Chinese diaspora in Africa totaling around half a million permanent residents.[131])

By the beginning of 2008 there were an estimated 800 Chinese corporations operating in Africa,[132] though the figure is undoubtedly higher by now.

Figure 17.2 on pages 94–95 shows just a few of the more important proposed Chinese investments in Africa for the short period of 2010 through part of 2012. This shows the countries and regions of Africa which have been given the most attention by China recently.

Although about half of China's imports of oil come from the Middle East, about one-third comes from African countries (Angola and at least 10 more countries).[135] Another one of these countries is the Sudan, where China continued pumping oil while the military equipment it provided to the Sudan government was used in its genocidal war against the people of Darfur.[136] Until 1993 China was self-sufficient in oil, or even a net exporter, but then it became an importer. In September 2013, China surpassed the U.S. and became the world's largest importer of oil.*

* The Council of Foreign Relations article referred to in this paragraph, from only a year and a half ago, cited a prediction that China would surpass the U.S. in oil imports by 2020. However, that actually happened in Sept. 2013 when China imported 6.30 million barrels while the U.S. imported only 6.24 million. [According

It is well to keep in mind that it has been the effort to grab and hold onto the world's oil supplies that has been the single most important impetus to the development of the endless wars of U.S. imperialism in recent decades. Can anyone seriously doubt that China will act any differently if it begins to fall to the Chinese military to defend *China's* imperialist access to foreign oil, rather than mainly the U.S. military?

The map in Figure 17.3 on pages 96–97 shows how pervasive China's oil and mineral rights in Africa have now become.

In addition to oil, Africa is very rich in minerals.† And China is now the world's largest importer of many important minerals. The Chinese economic penetration of Africa extends far beyond just oil and minerals, but they remain an extremely important reason why China is so rapidly expanding its presence in Africa.

In 2006 a journalist from the *Guardian* (U.K.) already wrote that:

> "China is driven by the same needs and compulsions that brought the Belgians to Congo, the British and the Dutch to South Africa, the Germans to Tanzania, the French to parts of the Sahara, and the Portuguese to Angola and Mozambique. The west had it once; now it is China's turn."[137]

Many other journalists and analysts now appropriately characterize China's activities in Africa in terms such as "voracious neocolonial pillaging".[138]

---

to the U.S. Energy Information Administration.] One of the reasons this occurred sooner than expected is that the U.S. is in the midst of a short-term oil production boom due to fracking. For now that means that U.S. oil imports are actually declining from year to year. But that will change again because fracked wells produce large quantities of oil for only a year or two. Within a decade or so the fracking boom will likely be over in the U.S. But even so, it is unlikely that the U.S. will ever catch up again to China in the amount of oil imported.

† "The African continent is home to around 30 percent of the world's total mineral reserves. It holds 42 percent of the world's bauxite, 38 percent of uranium, 42 percent of gold, 88 percent of diamonds, 44 percent of chromite, 82 percent of manganese, 95 percent of vanadium, 55 percent of cobalt and 73 percent of platinum." —"A Chinese investment view on mining in Africa", *Business Report* (Zambia), June 9, 2013, online at: http://www.iol.co.za/business/opinion/columnists/a-chinese-investment-view-on-mining-in-africa-1.1529523#.UfmbfKxsjms

Figure 17.2 Chinese Investment Offers in Africa Since 2010[133]

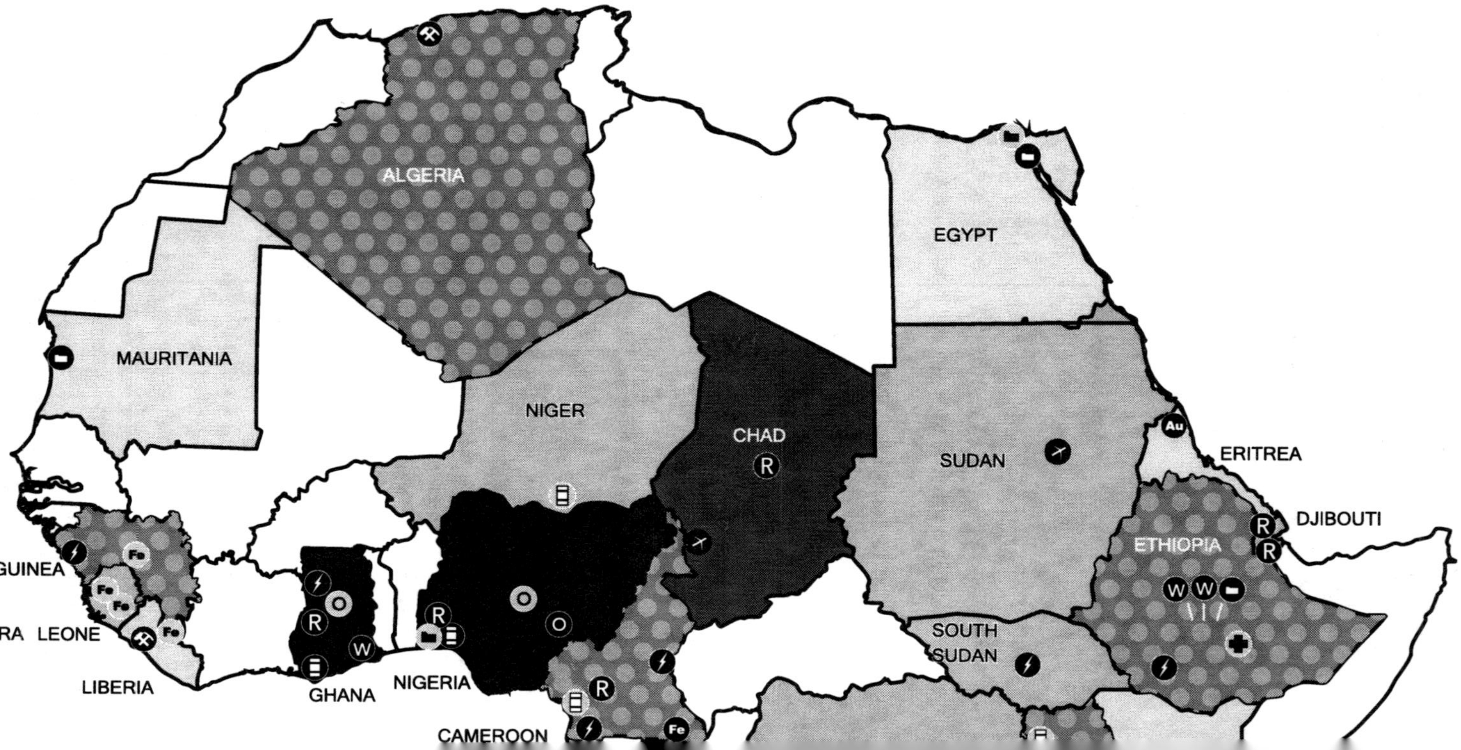

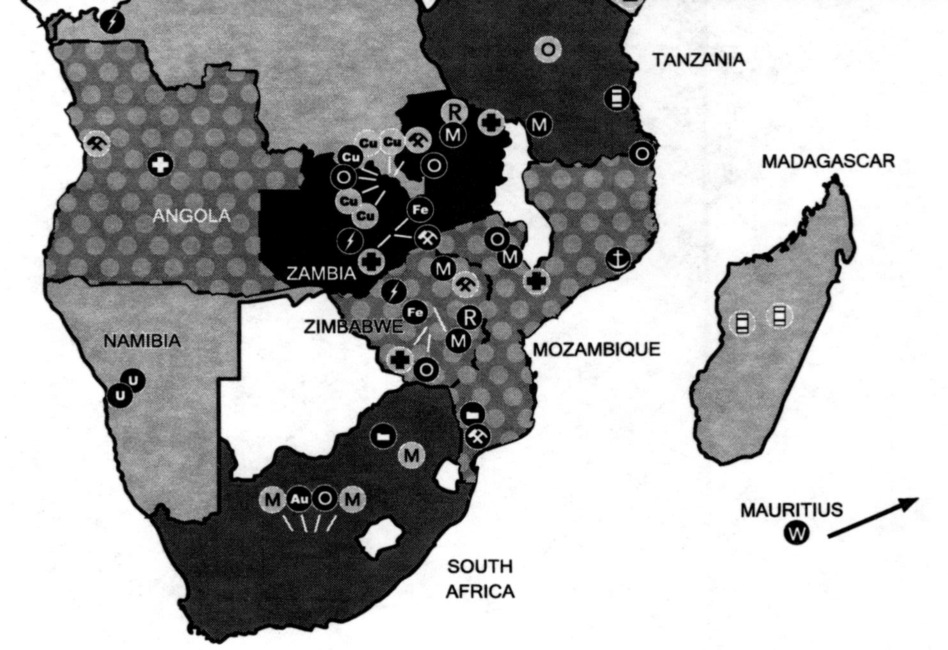

ESTIMATED OFFERS

- Less than $500 million
- $500 million to $1 billion
- $1 billion to $5 billion
- $5 billion to $10 billion
- More than $10 billion

* Estimated offer total: $101 billion

PERCENT OF CHINESE INVESTMENT BY SECTOR

- Oil and natural gas 19%
- Railroad 18.55%
- Other mining 10%
- Hydroelectric dams 9.2%
- Iron ore 7.4%
- Copper 6.9%
- Civil construction 5.9%
- Manufacturing 3.7%
- Uranium 2.3%
- Airports 2%
- Aid 1.8%
- Port construction 1.6%
- Gold 0.7%
- Water 0.5%
- Other 10%

Grey circles with black logos indicate completed

Figure 17.3 African Countries
Where China now has Oil or Mineral Rights[134]

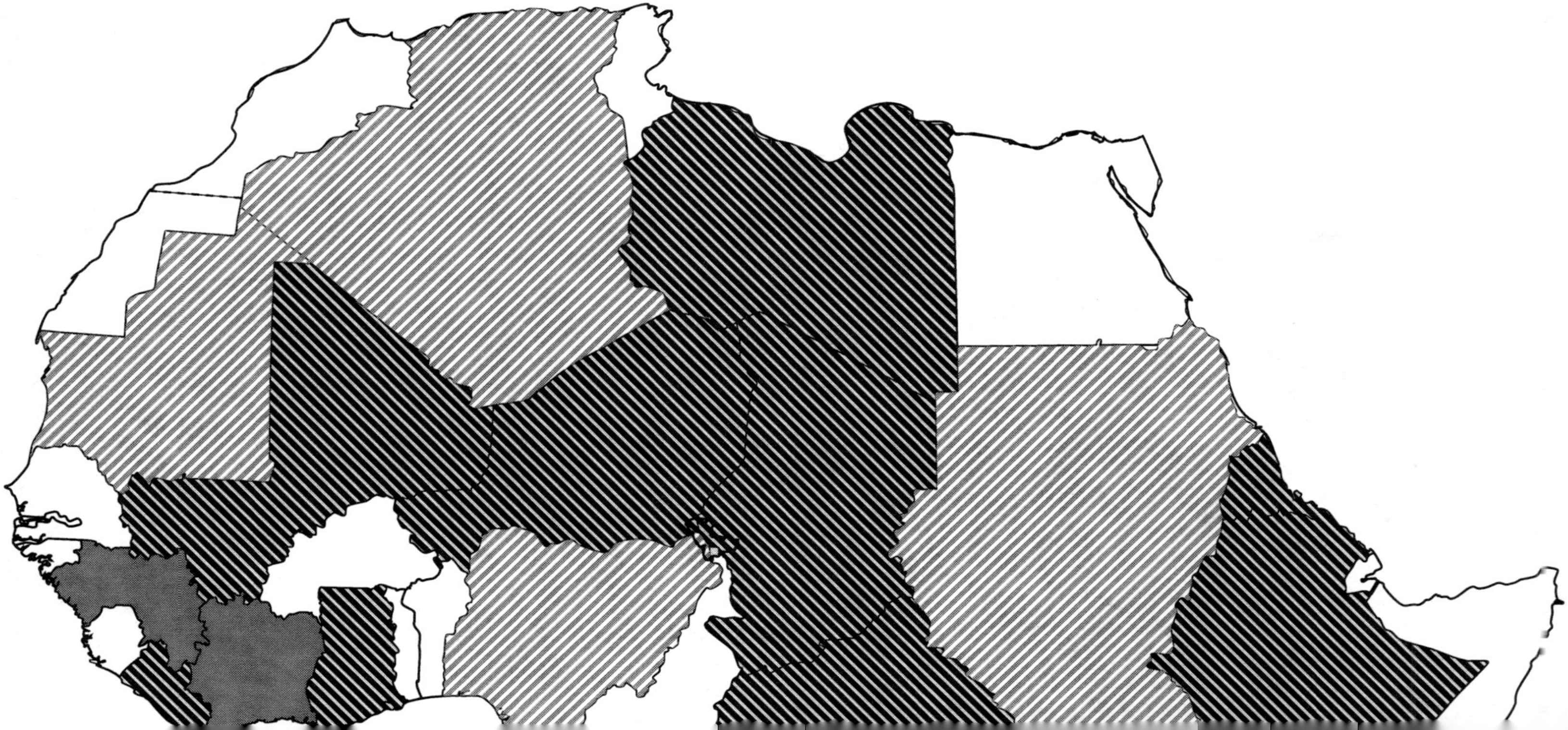

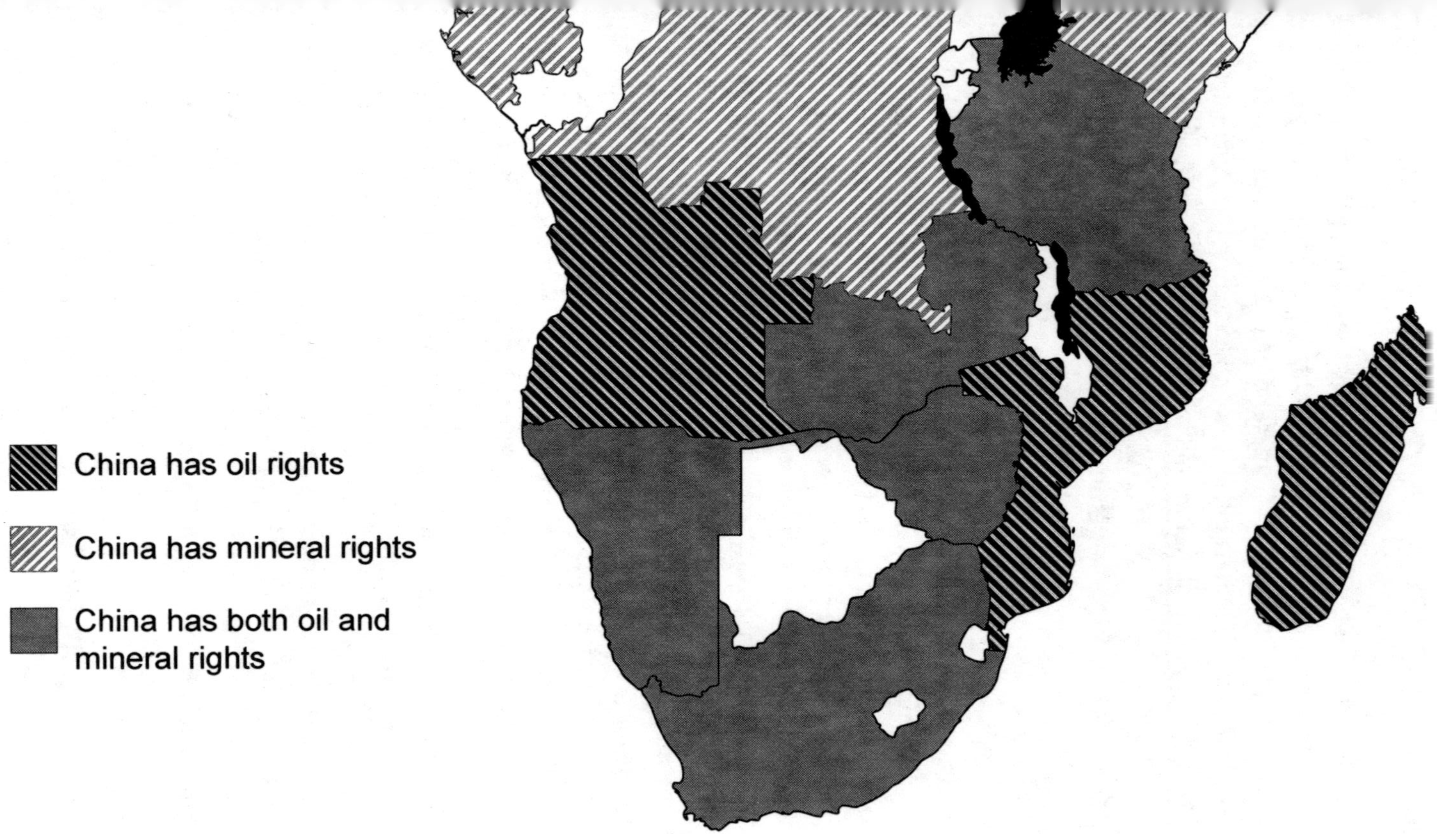

China has oil rights

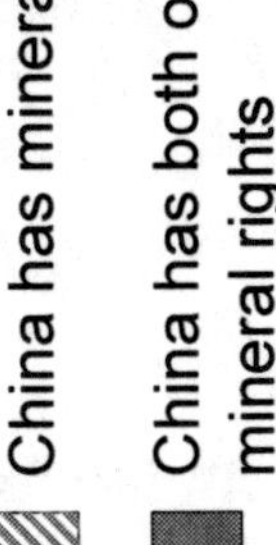
China has mineral rights
China has both oil and mineral rights

Some of the Chinese economic operations and practices in African countries have really been quite outrageous, even by prevailing imperialist standards. Many Chinese companies, and even tens of thousands of private Chinese citizens, are now pouring into Africa in something like a gold rush frenzy, and sometimes quite literally that!

In early June 2013 Ghana said it would expel 166 Chinese citizens who were detained over the past week in the country's gold-producing regions. Many of them lacked permits and were engaged in illegal mining and also prostitution. "If you have gold, then Chinese want to go there to mine it—it's like the American gold rush," He Wenping, the director of the African Research Section at the Chinese Academy of Social Sciences, said from Beijing. "Many times they are not clear about Ghana's laws since there are middlemen who bring them over and help them sign a contract." Illegal mining by Chinese has angered farming communities in Ghana because drinking water is being widely polluted. There is also resentment from the independent Ghanaian miners who can only afford to use shovels and pickaxes whereas the Chinese mines frequently employ high end industrial machinery and excavators.[139]

A couple years ago in Zambia the Chinese managers of a coal mine shot two Zambian employees who were protesting their low pay, which caused tremendous anger across the country.[140] In February 2013, the Zambian government revoked the mining license for a Chinese-owned coal mine after workers there rioted the previous November and killed a Chinese manager. The Zambian government said the mine had failed to comply with at least 15 laws.[141]

The governor of Nigeria's central bank, Lamido Sanusi, in an article in the *Financial Times* (London), recently noted that "China is no longer a fellow underdeveloped economy—it is the world's second-biggest, capable of the same forms of exploitation as the West. It is a significant contributor to Africa's de-industrialization and underdevelopment", because of its flood of cheap manufactured goods now rushing into Africa.[142] There is a "whiff of colonialism" about China's approach to Africa, he said.[143]

In Sudan and Ethiopia rebel groups have killed Chinese workers because they view them as being closely connected with the local government.[144]

This growing disgruntlement about the activities of many Chinese companies in Africa has led the Chinese government to try to "improve its image on the continent" through "foreign aid" and in various other ways, including "by financing the rapid expansion of Chinese media outlets across the continent to counter negative images of China and Africa with upbeat stories."[145]

Chinese "foreign aid" to Africa is substantial (perhaps as much as $3 billion this past year), and in 2009 45.7% of the Chinese aid budget went to Africa. In fact, there is in China some considerable public feeling that it should not be aiding other countries so much when it has so many poor people itself![146] (This is similar to right-wing ignorance and the typical sorts of complaints in this country about American "foreign aid" to the rest of the world.) These complaints assume that Chinese "foreign aid" actually constitutes strings-free gifts sent to foreign peoples, and fail completely to understand that this "aid" is actually for the purpose of promoting the Chinese economic exploitation of Africa.

Even if a portion of imperialist foreign "aid" ends up actually helping the people in the target country, overall it is really more like bribery on behalf of the corporations of the country sending that "aid".[147] One large part of Chinese "foreign aid" to Africa goes to government leaders and officials directly, or to their children for university study in China.[148] This is in effect for the purchase and training of future compradors. Another large part of Chinese foreign "aid" to Africa is in the form of loans, which are most often at market rates.[149] (This, as we mentioned earlier, is itself simply another method of exporting capital.)

18. China's rapid growth in military power.

China has been rapidly expanding its military power, and in particular it has been expanding it in ways which will enable it to exercise *its own* imperialist military intervention into other countries in the future. It understands full well that the maintenance of the present world imperialist system depends to a large degree on U.S. military power, and—unlike many other imperialist countries which really have little choice in this matter—China is unwilling to accept this reliance on a permanent basis.

A recent book by the Western journalist Geoff Dyer put it this way:

> "To keep its economy humming, China feels it needs to start molding the world it is operating in. China's economy relies on the continued safety of seaborne trade—something which has been guaranteed since the end of the Second World War by the navy of the United States, the country which the Chinese elite mistrusts the most (with the possible exception of Japan). Like other great powers before it, China is building a navy to take to the high seas because it does not want to outsource the security of its economic lifelines to someone else."[150]

For "the safety of seaborne trade", he says! That's a very disingenuous way of putting it even though there are actually a few pirates operating in Southeast Asian waters and in the Indian Ocean. By far the biggest threat to the transfer of wealth from the rest of the world to the ruling bourgeoisies of the major imperialist powers comes not at sea, but rather ultimately from the revolutionary masses *within* the countries whose wealth is being looted! The primary peacetime role of imperialist military power is not to "protect the sea lanes" but to keep exploited countries open for further foreign exploitation. But Dyer is correct to say that China is doing its very best to rapidly improve its military forces (naval and otherwise) so that it no longer needs to "outsource" this task to the U.S. and other imperialist countries.

Let's start by examining the rapid and consistent growth of Chinese military expenditures.

In talking about military expenditures in the world today the first thing to note is that U.S. military expenditures remain *huge*! A few years ago, U.S. spending on the military almost matched that of the entire rest of the world combined! As the Iraq and Afghanistan wars have wound down, the share of U.S. military spending in the world has dropped to 40%—which, of course is still enormous. No other country comes close.

And yet, what are the *trends* in world military spending today? Figure 18.1 below shows the 2012 military expenditures for a number of important countries and also the growth (or decline) rates for their military budgets for the 2011–2012 one-year period and for the 2002–2012 ten-year period.

For the one year period of 2011 to 2012 U.S. military spending dropped by 6.0% while China's increased by 7.8% and Russia's increased by 15.7%. But much more instructive is what has happened

Figure 18.1: Military Expenditures in Selected Countries (2012)[151]

In billions of constant 2012 U.S. dollars

Country	Expenditures	% of World Total	% Growth in Past Year	% Growth in Past 10 Years
United States	$682.478	40.0	- 6.0	49.9
China	$166.107	9.5	7.8	198.3
Russia	$90.749	5.2	15.7	126.1
U.K.	$60.840	3.5	- 0.8	12.4
Japan	$59.271	3.4	- 0.5	- 2.4
France	$58.943	3.4	- 0.3	- 0.4
Saudi Arabia	$56.724	3.2	15.8	112.1
India	$46.125	2.6	- 2.8	69.1
Germany	$45.785	2.6	0.9	- 2.9
Italy	$34.004	1.9	- 5.1	- 17.9
Brazil	$33.143	1.9	- 0.5	24.4
Australia	$26.158	1.5	- 4.0	31.0
Canada	$22.547	1.3	- 3.1	38.6
Turkey	$18.184	1.0	1.2	- 11.6
Israel	$14.638	0.8	2.5	- 10.0
Spain	$11.535	0.7	- 12.9	- 18.2
South Africa	$4.470	0.3	4.1	14.7
World Total	**$1,750.000**	--	**- 0.5**	--

over the last decade: Over that period U.S. annual military expenditures increased by nearly 50% (mostly because of its wars in Iraq and Afghanistan). Russia's military spending went up by 126.1%, which reflects the fact that Russian imperialism has been getting back on its feet after the final disastrous collapse of the state-capitalist Soviet Union in 1991. But by far the largest and most consistent increases in military spending on a regular yearly basis have been in China. Its expenditures went up by an amazing 198.3% over the past decade. Or putting it another way, China's annual military spending in 2012 was just short of *3 times* what it was as recently as 2002!

Year after year China increases its military budget by percentages that no other country, including the U.S., can afford. In other words, it is continually gaining military strength in comparison to the U.S. and other countries, though the U.S. (and perhaps also Russia) are still militarily stronger overall.

And, once again, we have to point out that even these statistics greatly understate the actual situation since they are based on official exchange rates. It costs a whole lot less in China to pay, feed, house and train a division of soldiers than it does in the U.S. And it costs a whole lot less to build a tank, jet airplane or missile submarine in China than it does in the U.S. If PPP conversion rates are used to convert Chinese military expenditures into dollars, China's military spending is substantially closer to that of the U.S. than the chart suggests.

But still, at present, China continues to be well behind the U.S. in military spending. However, as we've said, the *trend* here is for China to fairly rapidly catch up to the U.S. If, as could well happen, the U.S. is forced to make some deep cuts in its military spending over the next decade and a half, because the developing economic crisis takes further turns for the worse, then China might catch up to or even surpass the U.S. in military spending during that period. (China will also be very negatively affected by the world capitalist economic crisis, but probably not as soon or as severely at first.)

In fact we are already seeing a significant new decline in U.S. military spending right now because of the Budget Control Act (more commonly referred to as the "sequester" on Federal government spending) that is now scheduled to lead to an additional cut of $500 billion in the Pentagon budget over the next 9 years in addition to the $487 billion in cuts already underway. Originally this was not meant to actually occur; the deal between the Democrats and Republicans included the Pentagon reductions only as a means to force the Republicans to eventually back off on cuts to other programs. But as the *Economist* magazine recently noted, "It turns out that Republicans hate taxes even more than they love the armed forces."[152]

On February 24, 2014, U.S. Secretary of Defense Chuck Hagel outlined the additional cuts in military spending planned for fiscal year 2015, and large cuts in troop strength—to a level of 440,000 active duty soldiers—which has not been seen since before World War II. These cuts include eliminating an entire fleet of Air Force fighter planes. Hagel called these cuts "difficult choices" that will change defense institutions for years to come, and also noted that even deeper cuts will be necessary if the sequestration plan continues in fiscal year 2016. The cuts assume that the U.S. will no longer become involved in major, prolonged wars to try to establish "stability" in neocolonial countries such as the recent super-expensive debacles in Iraq and Afghanistan.[153]

It thus appears that the continuing U.S. budget crisis and U.S. and world economic crisis will be forcing continued reductions in U.S. military spending for years to come.

In European countries too this is happening, and there have been recent indications that other NATO countries will not only refuse to fund more of the massive costs of NATO (as the U.S. has been pleading for), but that many of them may actually further cut their own existing levels of funding. NATO funding by the top seven European contributors—the U.K., Germany, France, Italy, the Netherlands, Poland and Spain—has already dropped by more than 10% since 2009. Some ruling class defense analysts are now saying that new military budget cuts and declining funding risks destabilizing NATO over the long term.[154]

A popular theory exists that the U.S. defeated the Soviet Union in its long Cold War struggle largely because it forced an ultra-expensive arms race on the Soviets which they just could not afford. This sup-

Figure 18.2: Comparative Military Forces[155]

	Active Forces (2011)	Reserves (2011)	Tanks (2012)	Total Aircraft (2012)	Heli-copters (2012)	Naval Ships (2012)	Aircraft Carriers (2012)	Sub-Marines (2012)	Nuclear Weapons
U.S.	1,477,896	1,458,500	8,325	15,293	6,665	290	10 (a)	71	Yes
Russia	1,200,000	754,000	2,867	4,498*	1,635*	224	1	58	Yes
China	2,285,000	800,000	7,950	5,048*	901*	972	1 (b)	63	Yes
India	1,325,000	1,747,000	3,555	1,962	620	170	1 (c)	15	Yes
U.K.	224,500	187,130	227	1,412	367	77	1 (d)	10	Yes
France	362,485	419,000	571	544	410	180	1	10	Yes
Germany	148,996	355,000	408	925	493	67	0	4	No
S. Korea	653,000	3,200,000	2,466	871	97	190	0	14	No
Italy	293,202	41,867	720	770	357	179	2	6	No
Brazil	371,199	1,340,000	469	822	254	106	1	5	No

Notes

Active forces & reserves do not include paramilitary forces, which are quite large in some countries.

* Early 2013 data.

(a) Plus 2 old carriers in reserve, 2 more under construction, and 1 more ordered (for delivery in 2025). However, the "sequester cuts", if they continue, may force the moth-balling of as many as 3 present U.S. carriers.

(b) More are planned. (At least 3 more are already under construction.)

(c) Plus 1 being rebuilt, and 2 more under construction (1 of which was launched in Aug. 2013).

(d) Plus 2 under construction.

posedly wrecked the Soviet economy and led to the collapse of the U.S.S.R. Actually, this is gross exaggeration of what happened. The more fundamental truth was simply that Soviet state capitalism, with its much higher degree of monopoly and intractable bureaucratic corruption and stagnation could simply not compete with Western-style monopoly capitalism *at all!* The Soviet workers were totally fed up with the system; their widespread bitter joke was that "We pretend to work, and they pretend to pay us!" In other words, it was not just the arms race that did in Soviet state capitalism and social-imperialism, but its generally even more moribund overall economic system.

In any case, it is sometimes argued today that a similar arms race between the U.S. and China could now be used to defeat this new Chinese imperialist upstart. The obvious flaw in that argument is that the Chinese economy—even with its higher degree of official state ownership of many corporations and its higher degree of state interference in its private economy than in the U.S.—is nevertheless clearly much more dynamic and successful than the comparatively more moribund U.S. economy! And while the neocons did think about attempting the same sort of arms race with China to try to defeat it, it looks like in practice China is pushing the same contest against the U.S. and with a much better prospect of eventual success.

Figure 18.2 on the opposite page provides some comparisons of the military strength of the 10 countries with the most powerful militaries. By this ranking, from a bourgeois website, China is already the third most powerful country militarily. (It may well actually have the second most powerful military.) It has the largest standing army, and the second largest number of tanks, airplanes and submarines.

There are two very different sorts of wars that a rapidly rising capitalist-imperialist country like China must prepare for: 1) an inter-imperialist war (directly against another powerful imperialist country); and 2) an imperialist war against a much weaker, probably economically less developed ("Third World") country. ("Proxy wars" between imperialist powers are generally variations on this second type, since they typically take place in less developed countries and involve combat by competing local forces each partially armed by the contending imperialist powers.)

Perhaps surprisingly, it is actually cheaper to prepare to fight an inter-imperialist war, or at least to build up a sufficient retaliatory capability that such a war becomes significantly less likely. By acquiring nuclear weapons, ICBMs,[156] nuclear attack and ballistic missile submarines, dangerous anti-ship missiles, anti-satellite capabilities, and so forth, China has very likely already forestalled the possibility of any direct full-scale war between it and any other imperialist country (meaning the U.S. especially) any time soon. Only in the most dire and desperate circumstances (which are by no means inconceivable) is such a direct, all-out nuclear war at all likely to break out between the China and the U.S. over the next couple decades.

China presently has only one aircraft carrier, the *Liaoning*, which is a refitted and improved carrier formerly belonging to Ukraine. However, a second carrier is being built in the Dalian shipyard, and should be ready in 2018. The third and fourth Chinese carriers are expected to be completed by 2020.[157]

Aircraft carriers may already be essentially obsolete in any full-scale inter-imperialist war.[158] The reason for this is that they have become so vulnerable to modern nuclear-weapon laden missiles and torpedoes. Russia produces two especially feared supersonic guided missiles, called the Klub (3M-54) and the Yakhont, which can be launched from land, aircraft, ships or submarines, which carry large warheads (meaning potentially nuclear warheads), and reach targets 300 km away.[159] China is one of several countries which has purchased these fearsome weapons (and is also no doubt working to produce them itself). Russia also produces a rocket-powered torpedo (which China probably also has) called the VA-111 Shkval ("Squall") with a range of 11 km and a speed above 370 kilometers/hour which cannot be dodged or stopped by U.S. warships—which means the only thing they can safely do is stay out of range.[160]

So why then do the imperialist powers have so many carriers, and why are most of these countries (including China) building more of them? It is because carriers are now actually primarily weapons that are useful in imperialist wars against much weaker, economically underdeveloped and exploited countries (the so-called "Third World"). Carriers are mobile airfields which allow their imperialist owners to bomb most parts of the world.*

Many other weapons systems are like this too—of much more use in imperialist wars against weak and less economically developed countries than against other imperialist countries possessing modern countermeasures to them. Drones (remotely controlled aircraft) are another good example, since they are usually easily shot down by opponents with advanced missile systems. It is no accident that China has been rapidly expanding its development and production of drone aircraft as well as building more carriers.

China first publicly demonstrated its drones in October 2009, during its National Day parade. As of 2011 it already had at least 280 operational drones that could be used for "intelligence, surveillance and reconnaissance missions, precision strike missions and electronic warfare" according to one U.S. military think tank report. China's drone program is apparently very sophisticated, and it might even have models which are superior to those the U.S. has been using to assassinate "terrorists" (and civilians!) in Afghanistan and the Middle East. The author of the study said of Chinese drone technology, "They're certainly far more advanced than I expected them to be. You get the impression they're doing very advanced, cutting-edge research."[161] And China, even more than the U.S. apparently, has been working toward building drones that might be able to survive under "contested" conditions (i.e., to evade air and missile attacks directed against them).[162]

The Chinese navy is also imbued with a "going out" perspective, which could prove very useful not only in defending China and reconquering Taiwan, but also in extending Chinese military power all around the world.

* There has been a recent boom in the construction of aircraft carriers by both imperialist and sub-imperialist countries. In an article about the launching of a new Japanese carrier named the *Izumo* (officially called a "destroyer", since Japan's constitution does not allow offensive warships), the *Economist* states that China is building "at least 2 more" carriers of a design similar to the one they already have. See the article "Wide-mouthed frog", *Economist*, Aug. 10, 2013, p. 35. India also recently launched the first of 2 carriers it has been building, as noted in the news brief "Carrier nation", *San Francisco Chronicle*, Aug. 13, 2013, p. A-2.

Figure 18.3: The First and Second Island Chains[163]

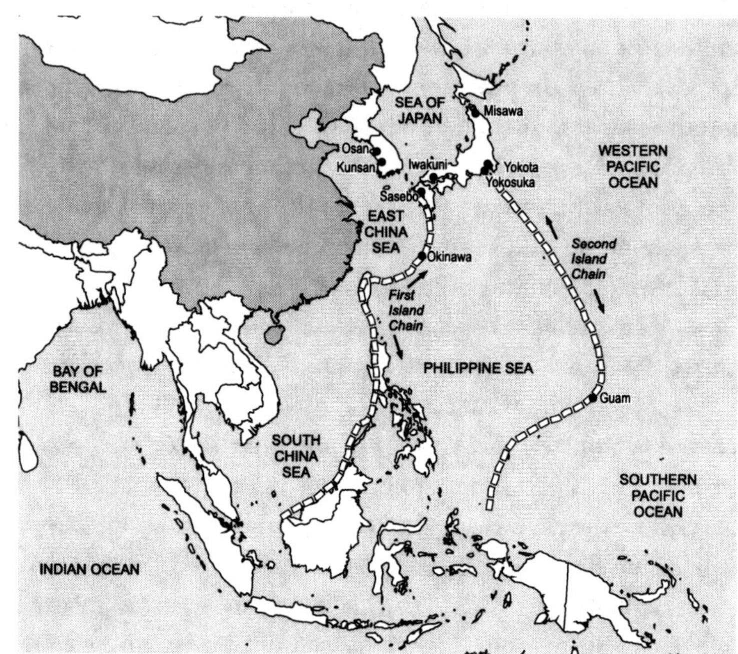

China's People's Liberation Army Navy (or "PLAN") was originally mostly a sort of coast guard operation (or "Brown-water navy"), but has become what is sometimes referred to as a "Green-water navy", that is, one which still does not usually stray very far from home. It is currently being transformed step-by-step into a "Blue-water navy" patrolling the oceans of the world, and supporting Chinese interests wherever they might be overseas. The PLA Navy is already patrolling the South China Sea and surrounding area out to the "First island chain" (Japan, Okinawa, the Philippines), and the next step will be to have it start regular operations out to the "Second island chain" (well out into the Pacific as far as Guam, Micronesia and Australia).[164] But the PLA Navy has already ventured even beyond this region at times, as for example into the Indian Ocean to "fight pirates" off of Somalia. It also sends its submarines into the Indian Ocean and elsewhere.

The Chinese military has also placed a major focus on Internet espionage and warfare. There have been many news reports over the past year about how semi-secret Chinese military units are stealing economic information from corporations around the world and passing it on to Chinese companies.[165] In this particular sphere, however, the military thrust is not directed against less developed countries, but is more of a form of inter-imperialist contention and economic struggle.

China is also making a major push to catch up to, and eventually surpass, the U.S. and Russia in space technology. In early June 2013 China sent its fifth manned space mission since 2003 into space, the Shenzhou 10 spacecraft with 3 astronauts, to test docking procedures with an experimental space lab already in orbit.[166]

The U.K. newspaper, the *Daily Mail*, in reporting this space flight, went on to note that China is still a long way behind the U.S. in space technology, but then added:

> "Still, the Shenzhou 10 mission will be the latest show of China's growing prowess in space and comes while budget restraints and shifting priorities have held back U.S. manned space launches.
>
> "China also plans an unmanned moon landing and deployment of a moon rover. Scientists have raised the possibility of sending a man to the moon, but not before 2020.
>
> "While Beijing insists its space programme is for peaceful purposes, a Pentagon report last month highlighted China's increasing space capabilities and said Beijing was pursuing a variety of activities aimed at preventing its adversaries from using space-based assets during a crisis.
>
> "Fears of a space arms race with the United States and other powers mounted after China blew up one of its own weather satellites with a ground-based missile in January 2007."[167]

On December 15, 2013, China accomplished that planned soft-landing of a rover on the moon, the first time this had been done by any country since 1976.[168] And while it is true that putting unmanned rovers on the moon was indeed done by both the U.S. and the Soviet

Union decades ago, the scientific community has been surprised by how sophisticated this new Chinese rover is and by the fact that it is doing important science.[169] This success moves the plan to put one or more Chinese astronauts on the moon a step closer.

There is even the possibility that China may try to be the first country to send a manned mission to Mars![170] But manned space travel is not the primary purpose of any nation's activities in space; it has much more to do with military issues. Satellites have become essential to military spying, GPS navigation, guidance for missiles, military communications, and in other ways. And the ability to destroy (or jam, or fool or take control of) an opponent's satellites has become a critically important aspect of war. In space, as on Earth, China is clearly preparing for a possible future showdown with the United States.

Finally, we should make note of the fact that while China is still behind the U.S. in military spending, and in various important ways in military power, we should also recognize that even from the military standpoint the U.S. is not as overpoweringly strong as is often supposed, and the rapid improvement in China's military power does not have as far to go in order to catch up with the U.S. as might be imagined.

First, it should be recognized that the U.S. military machine is tremendously bloated! It has large numbers of bases in the U.S. and over 1,000 bases overseas—many of which it doesn't really need, and serve little military purpose.[171] Many of the bases at home are maintained only to keep Congressmen happy (because of the money spent in their districts). In the same sort of way, many military weapons programs are extremely wasteful, or not even very useful. Again, the primary (hidden) purpose of many of these programs is actually "military Keynesianism"[172]—attempting to keep the U.S. economy going in a way that even Republicans (who are opposed to most government spending) generally support. For reasons such as this, the *militarily effective* portion of the U.S. military budget is only a part of the whole.

Second, there is the whole "fight the last war" syndrome which is so common among established military powers. A lot of the weaponry the U.S. has is actually of questionable military value for the types of wars that are occurring and are likely to occur in the future. For example, while the U.S. has been making military use of *a few* aircraft carriers in recent decades, most of them have been kept in service for a war that may never happen—and if it does happen, they are likely to be soon sunk by advanced weaponry already in the hands of potential enemies like China and Russia. For China to actually "catch up" militarily to the U.S. it *simply does not need* 10 aircraft carriers!

Third, most discussion of "China catching up militarily to the U.S." is focused on the scenario of a future interimperialist war between the U.S. and China. While such an all-out nuclear war could indeed happen eventually, for at least the next decade the more relevant question is how soon will China's own military be able to start acting in a more direct and powerful way to support the Chinese imperialist exploitation of as much of the world as it can (and in the same way that the U.S. military does)? And *that* is not very long in the future at all! The Chinese military is very rapidly catching up to the U.S. military with respect to the ability to protect its overseas investments and to bully other less developed countries.

However, China—like the U.S.—will inevitably find that militarily pacifying the world to facilitate its own imperialist economic exploitation of it is not so easy to do! There will be resistance to, and rebellions against, neocolonial regimes that China is attempting to prop up just as there has always been such resistance and rebellions against the regimes the U.S. and other imperialist powers have established and sought to protect. China, even as it succeeds in building an imperialist expeditionary power to patrol the world, will also inevitably get bogged down in imperialist wars in the same way that the U.S. has been in Vietnam, Iraq and Afghanistan.

19. China has already been involving itself in imperialist military activity.

There are various ways that China *already* intervenes militarily in other countries back here on Earth that we have not yet mentioned.

Thus while China does not itself yet engage in major imperialist wars in other countries (at least in any significant ways), it has already begun to involve itself militarily in civil wars and rebellions in other countries. It has usually actively supported established governments in their efforts to put down rebellions, but in at least one case (that we will discuss in a moment) it has actively supported the rebels in their efforts to overthrow an existing government and to replace it with a new regime more to China's liking. This is the sort of thing the imperialists call a favorable "regime change", and the U.S. and most other imperialist countries have done time after time.

China has been intervening in military conflicts around the world, and especially in Africa, through political and diplomatic support, through military advice and instruction (supplied by Chinese military attachés in foreign embassies, etc.), through military training of foreign personnel in China, and most of all by selling, or otherwise supplying, military weapons to the side it favors. Of course these are the sorts of things that all imperialist countries do, even the most "peaceful". But the point is that China is no different, has already become one of the most active imperialist countries in doing these sorts of things, and is rapidly ramping up these kinds of activities.

China has recently become one of the world's leading arms exporters. In March 2013 the Stockholm International Peace Research Institute issued a report noting that China had become the third largest arms exporter in the world in 2012. Over the past 10 years China has more than tripled its arms exports, rising from the world's seventh largest arms exporter in 2002 to third now.[174] Both Russia and the U.S. still export more than three times the annual value of arms that China does, so China is unlikely to pass either one of them for some years yet. But China is already starting to take away arms deals from other imperialist countries, especially Russia, but also including the U.S.[175]

Chinese will be able to tip the playing field in a way that will really hurt the operations of American multinational corporations."[88]

While not on the same scale of investment as in these major countries, China has also been buying up companies and resources in many smaller countries, all around the world. We will talk about its huge thrust into Africa in a separate section below, but China is also exporting capital heavily to Asian and Latin American countries and raiding their natural resources in a truly voracious way. We will just briefly mention a few example countries here by way of illustration of the general trend.

Laos, just south of China's Yunnan province, is one of the poorest and most backward countries in the world. One-third of the country is still contaminated with unexploded American bombs left over from the endless carpet-bombing of the country during the U.S. war against the people of Indo-China. Hundreds of people each year still lose limbs when they come across cluster bombs. But after this American devastation of the country, Laos is now suffering a new kind of devastation caused by Chinese investment and plunder, especially in the north of the country, and to a lesser extent by Vietnamese investment. The country is being systematically stripped of its timber and mineral resources.[89]

The deforested area in Oudom Xai province and other areas of the northern part of Laos is now so large that it is being monitored from space by Swedish researchers. It is causing serious soil erosion, loss of biological diversity and is forcing large numbers of multi-ethnic poor people off the land—probably into urban slums in Laos's capital Vientiane and a few other cities. A larger area of Laos is now owned by foreign investors (such as in Chinese-owned rubber plantations) than is devoted to rice farming in this very rural country![90]

In order to better move lumber, rubber, food crops, minerals and other goods north from Laos, China is building a $7.2 billion railroad from Kunming in Yunnan to Vientiane. This line is being financed by China's Export-Import Bank, and about 50,000 workers (including at least 20,000 Chinese workers) are doing the job. How Laos will be able to pay for this rail line is hard to imagine, given that its *entire* GDP was only around $9.4 billion in 2012![91]

lion; the 2010 purchase of 15% of the AES Corporation, one of the world's leading electrical power companies; the purchase of the Goss Corporation in 2010, a major manufacturer of printing presses; the purchase of GM's Nexteer Automotive unit in 2010 for $450 million; and many other substantial deals.[80]

Moreover, recently Chinese corporations and also individual rich Chinese investors have started buying U.S. real estate in a major way.[81] Some of these individual investments are huge! In October 2013 Fosun International, a Chinese conglomerate, agreed to buy a skyscraper near Wall Street for $750 million.[82]

Even more recently, Lenovo announced the purchase of Motorola from Google for $2.9 billion. Many view this purchase as being in considerable part for the acquisition of a well-known Western brand name as well as to expand further into the mobile phone market.[83] Also in January 2014 Lenovo announced the purchase of IBM's low-end computer server business for $2.3 billion.[84]

There will likely be a much bigger surge of Chinese direct investment, and also portfolio investment in private companies, into the U.S. very soon. One major reason is that China is tired of just investing vast amounts of its foreign reserves in U.S. Treasury securities that presently pay extremely low rates of interest (because the Federal Reserve continues to flood the financial system with more money). The State Administration of Foreign Exchange (SAFE), the Chinese government agency which oversees foreign reserve investments, recently established an office in Manhattan to make alternative U.S. investments promising higher rates of return. This new office is separate from the office that buys U.S. government debt, and will focus on buying private equity, real estate, and other U.S. assets.[85] This follows a similar program already begun in Britain.[86]

Just how big will Chinese FDI in the U.S. get? One private research company, the Rhodium Group, estimates that by 2020—just five years away—it will balloon to between $100 billion and $400 billion.[87]

These rapidly expanding Chinese purchases of American companies are already raising major concerns within both the U.S. government and U.S. corporations that compete with China. "With every company they purchase, every piece of technology they get, the

Figure 19.1: World's Leading Arms Exporters[173]

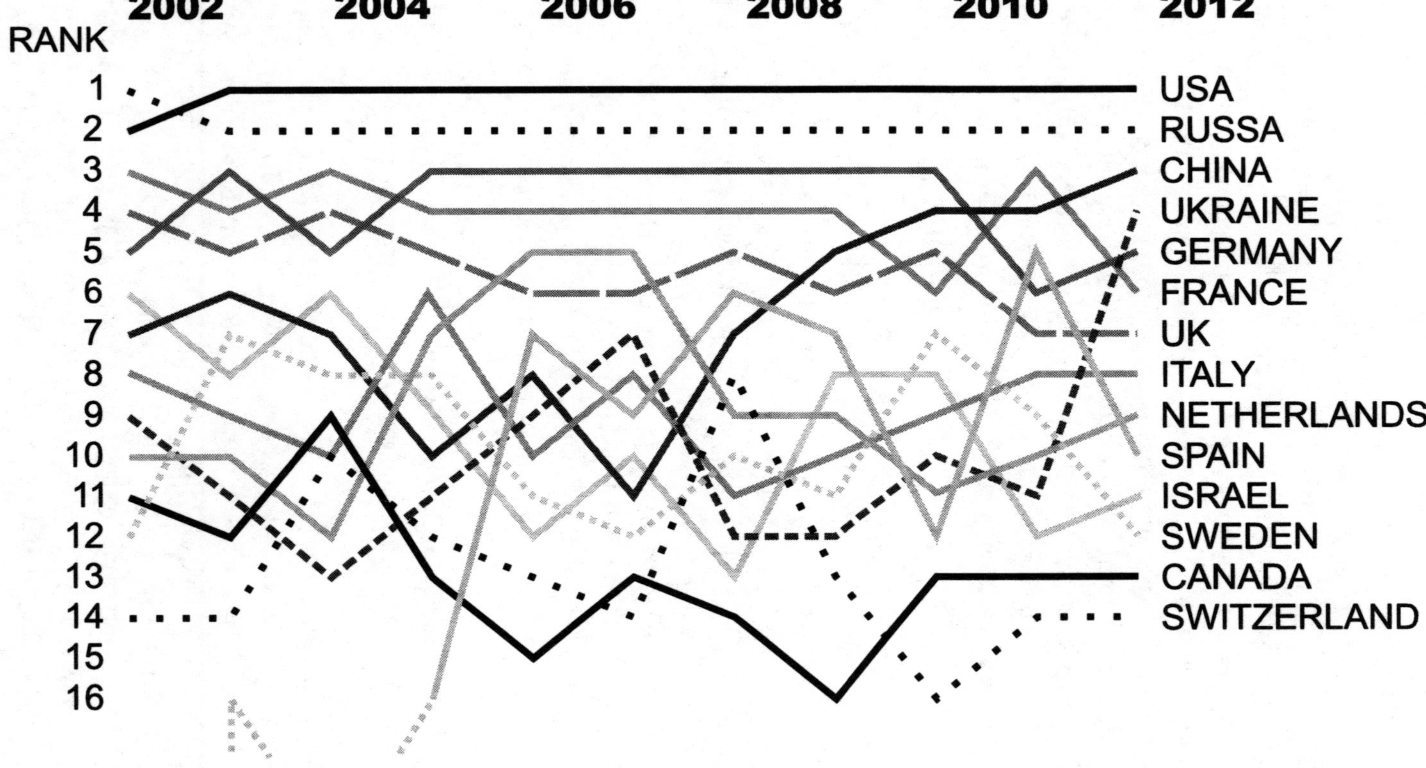

In 1990 China agreed to join in "UN peace-keeping responsibilities". Small numbers of Chinese troops have been sent on these missions to Liberia (2005), the Western Sahara, Sierra Leone, the Ivory Coast, and the Democratic Republic of Congo.[176] China seems to have mixed feelings about such operations; on the one hand it is anxious to get some foreign military experiences of this sort, but on the other hand it is trying to keep a low profile so as not to appear to Africans as just another colonialist power interfering in the internal affairs of African countries.

However, China has on at least one occasion already provided military support to try to overthrow an African regime which didn't sufficiently support its interests:

> "China has put its weight behind the conflict in Chad. The FUC rebellion based in Sudan and aiming to overthrow the pro-Taiwan ruler of Chad, Idriss Déby, has received Chinese diplomatic support as well as light weapons and Sudanese oil. With Sudan maintaining a pro-Chinese stance, and Chad being pro-Taiwan (and since 2003, an oil producer), China has pursued their interests in replacing Déby with a more pro-China leader. The 2006 Chadian coup d'état attempt failed after French intervention, but Déby then switched his support to Beijing, with the apparent defeat becoming a strategic victory for China."[177]

China has military alliances with at least 6 African countries, including Sudan, Algeria, Nigeria and Egypt. It has military attachés at its embassies in many countries, and many countries have military attachés at their embassies in Beijing. China provides military training for the arms it sells, and more general forms of military training for officers from other friendly regimes, though in many ex-colonial countries (now neocolonial) it is still behind the former owners of these colonies—such as Britain and France—in providing such military training and services.[178]

20. "Imperialism with Chinese Characteristics"

Almost everyone in the world knows by now that China is no longer a socialist country. Even the capitalists in the West, and the U.S. government, have long since come to recognize this full well—despite their continuing criticism that China is ruled by what is still called a "Communist" Party. (However, even western ideologists now criticize the CCP not for being *communist*, but rather for being *authoritarian.*)

But the CCP itself, and the Chinese government, still try to keep up the pretense that the country is "socialist". According to them the Chinese system today is "socialism with Chinese characteristics". The Chinese ruling bourgeoisie fears that openly admitting the obvious—that China is a capitalist country ruled by its own capitalist class centered in the CCP—would destroy whatever lingering "legitimacy" that they think they have. Hence the continuing absurd verbal pretense.

Only a few revisionists, in China and elsewhere, have failed to understand this basic situation.*

* The only people who are even still partially fooled by the claim that China is "socialist" are those who are so benighted and confused that they believe that having many state owned enterprises (SOEs) is the "same thing" as socialism. However, if the state is controlled by the bourgeoisie acting in its own class interests, then the existence of any state-owned or nationalized corporations actually means there is a *state capitalist* sector of the economy, which is not real socialism by any stretch of the imagination. State capitalist corporations are those owned and controlled by the bourgeoisie as a whole (as a class), as opposed to "private" corporations which are owned by individual groups of capitalists. Revisionists, however, are always prone to confusing state capitalism with socialism.

In China, moreover, the SOEs largely operate as if they were private corporations, and state ownership does not prevent such operation—and in many cases enhances it. State ownership does not exempt SOEs from their focus on capitalist market forces and the perpetual pressures for greater enterprise profitability. On the other hand, the Chinese state very actively gives general direction to (or "interferes in") the whole economy, including both SOEs *and* private corporations. But this sort of partial merger of the bourgeois state with the corporations is a general feature of capitalism in the modern imperialist era, and applies to every single capitalist country to one substantial degree or another.

Consequently, all around the world (and maybe even for growing numbers of people within China itself), this phrase "socialism with Chinese characteristics" is viewed humorously, as the ridiculous nonsense that it clearly is. And this has led to the tag "with Chinese characteristics" being tacked onto other features of contemporary China whenever an element of humor or ridicule is desired.

A case in point is the small book by Michael Metcalf, *Imperialism with Chinese Characteristics?*, which was published in 2011 by the National Intelligence University operated by the Department of Defense of the U.S. government.[179] Metcalf is a faculty member of the NIU and has spent decades working for the Defense Intelligence Agency and the State Department's Bureau of Intelligence and Analysis. His special focus is in helping the U.S. government and military understand the actual motivations and intentions of the Chinese government and the CCP.

Metcalf's central thesis is that China is now an imperialist country (though perhaps with "Chinese characteristics") and that it is rapidly preparing its military to protect and promote Chinese imperialist economic interests abroad.

It probably seems quite bizarre to many people that anyone in the U.S. military or government would condemn China for being *imperialist* or for building up a military force capable of protecting and expanding its foreign economic interests! After all, the U.S. since World War II has itself been the most powerful imperialist country in the world, engaged in constant economic and political intervention into other countries and almost constant wars to protect and expand its own politico-economic interests! And since the collapse of the Soviet Union the U.S. has been the sole superpower, the unquestioned top dog among all the imperialist powers.

And yet, it is the top imperialist dogs themselves who are most alert to, and afraid of, the rise of new imperialist competitors. They know very well what they themselves are doing in the world, and they really don't like it one bit when they see other countries rising to challenge them in doing the very same thing, especially if those upstart imperialists threaten to go outside the existing, agreed upon framework of a single imperialist system with established "rules"!

With a mixture of both extreme greed and hopes for major new profits (on the one hand), but also trepidations about the rise of a potential new capitalist-imperialist competitor (on the other hand), the U.S. and other long-established imperialist countries gradually accepted China into the current world imperialist system over the past 25 years. The key event which formalized China's joining the world imperialist system was its acceptance into the World Trade Organization in December 2001, after long and arduous negotiations.*

As we have argued earlier, China is now not only an integral part of the current world imperialist system, it has even come to play an indispensible role within that system (as the primary super-exploited "workshop of the world", and through its support of the world financial system via its purchase of massive runaway government debt in the U.S. and other imperialist countries).

But China is also a major *threat* to that current world imperialist system if it gets so powerful economically (and eventually militarily) that it is able to rewrite the rules of that existing system in its own favor, or else if (what is far more likely) it becomes strong enough to

* China became a member of the WTO on Dec. 11, 2001. The U.S. and other dominant members of the WTO insisted on many concessions by China and even substantial changes to its internal economic laws and structure, which is why the negotiations dragged on for so many years. In the early 1980s China began to open up its economy to foreign investment (at first just in Special Economic Zones), and signed a number of regional trade agreements. China obtained observer status with GATT (the predecessor to the WTO) and in 1986 began its efforts to join that organization as a full member. The U.S., Europe and Japan insisted that China become essentially a complete capitalist market economy, on major tariff reductions, and on changes to its industrial policies before it was allowed to join. These changes forced China to considerably revise its basic economic strategy and policies, and meant that China would have to agree to the existing rules of global capitalist trade and competition even though it had no part in making those rules. The ruling class in China decided to take a chance on doing this, and this bet has paid handsomely for them (from a bourgeois perspective!).

Since joining the WTO China has become much more deeply integrated into the world capitalist economy. The U.S. and other older imperialist countries have benefitted tremendously from China's entrance into the WTO and its more general full entrance into the world imperialist system. But capitalist China has benefited the most, and has emerged as a very dangerous capitalist-imperialist competitor to the U.S. and other imperialist countries.

split off part of that imperialist system into an independent (or semi-independent) imperialist system that China itself dominates. This is the possibility *and trend* that so alarms the U.S. ruling class!

Michael Metcalf bases his analysis of China's military intentions not primarily on China's continuing rapid expansion of its military spending and power (which of course both he and the U.S. government in general are very well aware of), but rather on some key writings of Chinese military and political leaders.

In particular, every two years since 1998 China has released a public "defense white paper" describing the overall role and strategy of China's military. Metcalf focuses on the 2006 White Paper and on two explanatory essays further explicating China's military thinking which were written by one of the main authors of those official white papers, Chen Zhou,[180] and which were published in the Chinese military journal, *China Military Science,* in 2007 and 2009.

Chinese military doctrine is quite clear that *military strategy* depends on what *political goals* are being aimed at. In the early decades of the People's Republic of China the central political goals were survival and warding off attack by foreign imperialism (the U.S. and the social-imperialist Soviet Union), both against China itself and also against other countries such as North Korea and Vietnam. But that basic security situation is now qualitatively different and vastly better for China. The Soviet Union collapsed, and Russia today is much weaker relative to China than it once was. Moreover, China now possesses nuclear weapons, ICBMs, nuclear powered missile submarines, and other military capabilities which prevent even the U.S. from launching any direct attack against it. As Chen Zhou puts it, "China's security environment on the whole is favorable, and there is no instant danger of large-scale foreign aggression against China."[181]

So what new political goals have now come to the fore, to serve as the primary determinant of the changing Chinese military strategy? Of course further strengthening of defenses against attack by other imperialist countries is still important, as is the long time goal of recovering Taiwan. But the new central goal added to these is that of *economic development.* Chen Zhou writes that reform and development now affects the overall national security. This is because "Reform and development is now at a critical stage and the contradictions and problems affecting social harmony and stability are increasing. China's economic dependence on the overseas markets is increasing, so the economic security is facing greater risks."[182] As Metcalf summarizes it, "The reader can see that, for Chen, security and development seem to be merging into one issue."[183]

For Chen Zhou and the entire Chinese ruling class, the perceived interests of the state have changed and broadened:

> "China's national defense always puts the state's sovereignty and security in the primary position, and always takes guarding against and resisting aggression, stopping armed subversion, defending the state's sovereignty, unity, territorial integrity and security as the basic tasks. **With the changes of the times and the development of the nation, the security interests and the development interests have been interwoven, the interests of one's own country have been closely linked with the interests of other nations, the gravity center of interests have [sic] shifted from survival to development, the form of realizing the national interests has extended from domestic to international,** the scope of the national interests has extended from the traditional territorial land, seas, and air to the maritime, space, and electromagnetic domains..."[184] [Emphasis added.]

Metcalf sums this up: "In other words, the new stage of development has caused the merging of development concerns and traditional territorial security concerns, and this has pushed China's state security interests offshore."[185] Chen Zhou also states:

> "The armed forces need to cope with traditional security threats, and also to cope with non-traditional threats; need to safeguard the state's survival interests, **and need to safeguard the state's development interests**; need to safeguard the homeland security, **and also to safeguard the overseas interests security**; need to safeguard the overall

> state interests of reform, development, and stability, and also need to safeguard world peace and promote common development."[186] [Emphasis added.]

Chen Zhou further states: "The military capability is the core of the state's strategic capability and should be able to be extended to wherever the state's interests develop to."[187]

In short, the Chinese military is being changed and "modernized" so that it can more easily operate in other countries where Chinese economic interests are at stake. This is straightforward imperialist thinking and strategy. If this isn't yet clear enough, let's quote some more of this new Chinese military strategy:

> "Today while the Chinese economy is increasingly merging into the global economic system and the state interests are continuously extending outward, China's national defense will assume a more active and open posture in moving into the outside world, will preserve the state interests in a broader sphere of domains beyond the limits of territory and sovereignty, and will provide military support and guarantee for the development interests."[188]

And again:

> "Development and security constitute an organic unified entity, in which development is the foundation for security, and security is the guarantee for development. Being the strong backup for the nation's security and development, national defense should strive to effect the combination of safeguarding both the security interests and the development interests. With China's connection to the outside world changing from a less close condition to a close condition, China's influence on the international community and the external obstruction that China will be facing will rise side by side, so the domestic security will more heavily influence the international situation, and the international security will more deeply influence the domestic situation

> as well. National defense should coordinate the domestic situation and the international situation... **...with the pace of 'stepping out' being quickened, the issue of protecting the overseas interests is getting increasingly prominent. National Defense should, from the high plane of economic globalization's development and safeguarding the state's economic security, effectively raise the capability of protecting our country's overseas interests, and ensure the protection of the overseas interests security while guaranteeing homeland security.**"[189] [Emphasis added.]

Hmmm. "Stepping out," this Chinese imperialist military strategist calls it. That used to mean going on a romantic date; now it apparently means the imperialist exploitation of the world, backed up when necessary by military force!

Chen Zhou goes on to state that "With China's full involvement in the process of economic globalization, the state's development interests will unavoidably go beyond the scope of the country's territory and will certainly be extended to other countries and regions."[190] But he is at pains (like any other imperialist ideologist) to try to justify this and explain why, in China's case, it will be done in the "common interests" of all the countries involved. This reminds us of Japanese imperialism's "Greater East Asia Co-Prosperity Sphere" claim of the 1930s. Imperialists always claim that their predations are in "everybody's best interests".

But what about China eventually setting up foreign military bases to maintain control of its developing economic empire, the way that U.S. imperialism does? These are also being planned and pre-justified. While claiming that China will never pursue a Western-style policy in this regard, Chen Zhou states in another article:

> "Therefore, though we resolutely oppose 'neo-interventionism' that 'puts human rights above sovereignty,' we cannot negate the overseas use of military for any defensive and humanitarian purposes. We must reserve our right to carry

> out legal 'intervention' or 'interference' when the nation's core overseas interests are being seriously jeopardized."[191]

And adds the following, indicating that China will indeed seek to establish foreign military bases:

> "As for whether or not military bases should be established in overseas areas, this is something related to our country's independent peaceful foreign policy and defensive national defense policy, and is also restricted by the national and military conditions, the comprehensive national power, and the path of development of our country... These conditions and characteristics and the fact that our military's strength are [sic] not yet commensurate with the requirement of the missions determine that we should act within our capacity in safeguarding our overseas interests, deal with issues case by case, and make steady advances... Even when we become really powerful in the future, we will still not establish a global network of military bases on a large scale like some countries do..."[192]

In other words, China will start with just a few foreign military bases, and see how many more become "necessary".

Michael Metcalf, the U.S. military analyst who brought this strategic imperialist thinking by the Chinese ruling class and military to public attention makes an additional quite valid point. It is true that China does *not yet* have any foreign military bases, and it is true that China has *not yet* engaged in any foreign imperialist wars (at least in the direct way that the U.S., or even Britain and France have done in recent decades). Metcalf describes China today as the land of the "not yet". He says:

> "If we choose to see current China's activity as no more than an add-on to last year's activity, we run the risk of missing the early stages of fundamental changes as well as the risk of seeing the future goals as merely additions to past goals... Thus, to fully appreciate present Chinese be-

> havior, it must be seen from the perspective of the future at which it aims. I believe that Chen's explanation of the 2006 Defense White Paper gives us that goal: a very powerful China active in the international arena, using its military strength to further and protect its interests and diplomacy, and with a series of military bases abroad to support those military missions. In other words, they intend imperialism with Chinese characteristics."[193]

Actually, from the Leninist point of view, China has been a capitalist-imperialist country for quite some time already, but it is true that the *military aspect* of this imperialist nature is still developing. Chinese military interventions in support of Chinese imperialist investments around the world have not been necessary so far (except on token levels) because of the existence of the world imperialist system wherein the U.S., with the support of a few other imperialist countries such as Britain and France, has been handling most of the war work. But China is not content with this arrangement and figures that it will be able to pull in a greater and more secure share of the world's wealth if it starts to rely more on its own military interventions to support its ever expanding imperialist economic penetration of the world.

However, we'll let Michael Metcalf continue with some of his summary:

> "The center of gravity of China's state interest has changed from China's survival to China's development. Therefore, the primary mission of China's military is no longer China's survival and territorial security but now is protecting and expanding China's developmental interests, wherever those interests might be located. This mission will require a much greater military force than was required when mere survival and territorial defense formed the core of China's state interests... So, the core of China's state interest has changed from mere survival to development—and this is a major event. It is a qualitative change and not a mere quantitative change. China has crossed a threshold.

> "Not long ago it was possible to reach a loose consensus on what military force China would require and develop. When survival was the primary objective, people's war could provide defense against a conventional invasion of China but not against a nuclear attack. Once China deployed a small but reliable nuclear force, China had assured its survival.... With development as the new core of state interest, the only limit to China's military needs will be the limit of China's developmental interests. But development interests seem to be of a type that constantly expands. Or is China of such a nature that one day it will declare that its development has reached its desired limits?
>
> "Unless one can predict the limit of China's development goals, one cannot predict the limit of China's military requirement. China plans to develop a military force commensurate with its economic status, with most analysts assessing that its status will surpass that of the United States by earlier than mid-century. But will China then stop? At present its military development lags behind even its current requirement. Therefore, for a very long time China's military development will be racing not only to catch up to its current requirement but also to prepare for future requirements that have no foreseeable limits."[194]

Indeed, for a rising imperialist power, especially one contending with an existing imperialist power possessing a powerful military machine, there is no such thing as having too much military strength!

Thus we see that "imperialism with Chinese characteristics" is still just imperialism. No matter how much red lipstick you smear on a pig's lips, it is still ... just a pig. And even if it is still only a young pig (from the military intervention standpoint), it is rapidly growing up to become a very wild and dangerous imperialist boar.

China has continued releasing its "defense white papers" in the years since 2006, but the later ones neither add much, nor show any significant changes in China's official views about the role and strategy of its military. If anything the more recent white papers have been couched in more abstract and less revealing terminology.[195]

However, someone might suppose that since China has not yet followed through on *some* of the key military goals and plans it outlined in earlier defense white papers, and in commentaries on them in Chinese military journals, that perhaps China does not really intend to implement them. In particular this question might be raised about the earlier discussions suggesting that foreign military bases could well be established at some point. As far as we know, no such foreign Chinese military bases have yet been established, though there are Chinese military attachés in many countries. Nevertheless, there have been continuing signs that they are definitely still being considered and even planned for.

In 2013 the small country of Djibouti in the Horn of Africa actually publicly offered China the option of establishing a military (probably naval) base in that country. The U.S., France and even Japan (!) already have bases there.[196] It is not yet known if China will actually establish a base there.

There have also been news reports over the past couple years that Pakistan has requested that China build its first overseas naval base there, and that Seychelles has made such a request as well. There was even a rumor that Iran would like to provide a small island in the Red Sea to China for a naval base. True or not, these reports and rumors are instructive and part of a growing pattern.[197]

There is continuing discussion of the "need" for such overseas bases in the Chinese media. The map below, from a Chinese government newspaper in 2013, shows 18 possible locations for PLA naval bases to protect China's "energy line" in the Indian Ocean area. Besides Djibouti Port, the locations suggested are: Chongjin Port (North Korea), Moresby Port (Papua New Guinea), Sihanoukville Port (Cambodia), Koh Lanta Port (Thailand), Sittwe Port (Myanmar), Dhaka Port (Bangladesh), Gwadar Port (Pakistan), Hambantota Port (Sri Lanka), Maldives, Seychelles, Lagos Port (Nigeria), Mombasa

Port (Kenya) Dar es Salaam Port (Tanzania), Luanda Port (Angola) and Walvis Bay Port (Namibia).

It is, of course, unlikely that China would receive permission from *all* these countries to create naval bases there at the present time, or even that it would immediately like to do so. Still, media reports like this do illustrate the serious thinking going on in China today about the need to establish foreign military bases, and the likelihood that at least some of them will be established fairly soon.

Figure 20.1: Chinese Media Discussion of Proposed Chinese Bases[198]

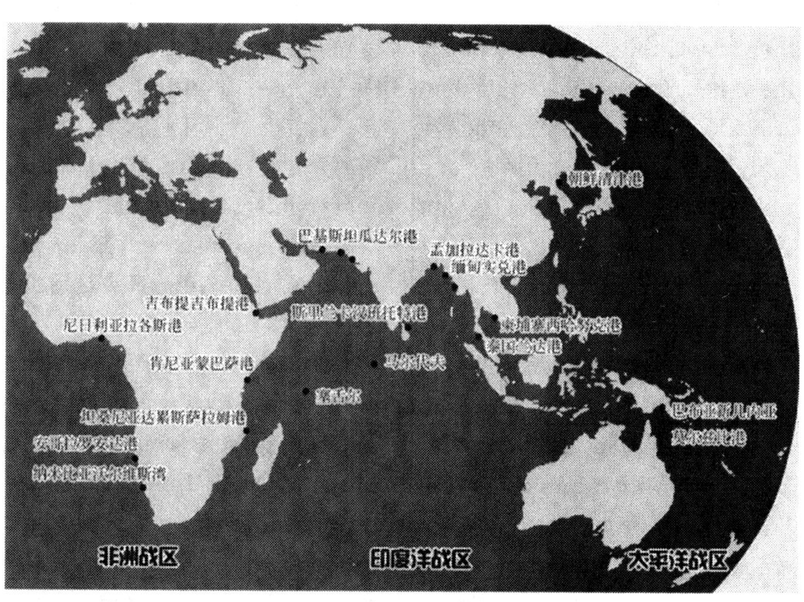

21. China's growing nationalism and belligerence.

With the expansion of China's economic and military strength we already see a growing nationalism and belligerence not only by the Chinese government, but also on the part of a section of Chinese public opinion—especially among the ruling bourgeoisie and the now quite large urban "middle class". This sort of thing is inevitable in any imperialist country, especially in one that is ambitious and still rising and growing continually stronger.

All this is illustrated very well in the disputes over various tiny islands in the South China Sea, disputes which have become much more serious in 2012–2014. There have been competing claims over the ownership of these islands (or in many cases just reefs occasionally protruding from the sea) for many decades. But in recent years these disputes have become much more heated. And why is that? It is primarily because China has begun pressing its claims much more strongly, sending its PLA Navy ships out to patrol the areas around these islands or rocks, setting up military installations on some of the larger islands, and so forth. The Philippines, Vietnam, Taiwan and others have in turn also escalated their own demands with regard to these islands and reefs, and sent out their own patrol boats. There is now the real possibility that there might develop one or more wars over these rocks!

These islands, or shoals, have little intrinsic value, but officially owning them also means owning the sea and sea-floor areas around them, out to as much as 200 miles with regard to economic exploitation. That means valuable fishing rights, and also potentially very important undersea oil, gas and mineral rights. So it is not just China's growing nationalism and assertiveness which is at work here, but also the desire of all these countries to secure new territories for economic exploitation, especially now that deep-sea oil drilling has become technologically feasible (if still very dangerous for the environment). But still, it has been China's new aggressiveness which has directly led to this sudden rapid escalation of demands and threats from all sides.

In addition, ownership of these islands and shoals means having the ability to establish forward radar sites and other military installations on them, and to better control the entire South China sea from a naval perspective. So while it may seem that all the fuss is just over "rocks" in reality there are much more important matters at issue.

On July 24, 2012, China unilaterally established the Sansha prefecture to "oversee and administer" one million square miles of the South China Sea. As of January 1, 2013, this oceanic prefecture was unilaterally invested by the Chinese government with the police authority "to board, seize and expel foreign ships" from this vast area.[199]

One such set of rocks in this "prefecture" is known as the Scarborough Shoal, which lies 115 miles from the Philippines coast. In the past year China sent a fleet of 90 ships to the area which have barred Filipino fishing boats from operating there. Similarly, China dispatched some naval frigates to the Ayungin Reef (also known as the "Second Thomas Reef"), which is 105 miles from the Philippines, to do the same thing. Control of the Ayungin Reef probably means control of the Recto Bank (underwater mounds in the sea) about 85 miles from the Philippine coast, which the U.S. Energy Information Administration estimates might contain 213 billion barrels of oil and 2 quadrillion cubic feet of natural gas.[200]

There have been numerous outraged comments about China's claims and encroachment on these islands from the Philippines. Some politicians there have called China's claim "the most brazen maritime grab in history" and stated that China's behavior "is that of an imperial state, imitating the expansionist conduct of the western powers it condemns". However, President Benigno "Noynoy" Aquino has been particularly agitated in his condemnations of China, saying that Western powers must tell China that "enough is enough", and comparing his country to Czechoslovakia being overrun by Nazi Germany in the period before World War II in Europe! [201]

There are many more islands, rocks, reefs or shoals which are lumped together, along with the reefs mentioned above, under the name of the Spratly Islands in the South China Sea. Some or all of these are claimed by not only China, but also by the Philippines, Malaysia, Taiwan, Vietnam and Brunei. And all of these countries except Brunei currently occupy and/or patrol some of these islands. (Many of the reefs are only above water at low tide.) The areas around these islands are also important for fishing and commercial shipping, and hold significant reserves of oil and natural gas. These islands too are part of China's "Sansha prefecture", but any attempt by China to force the other countries completely out of the area may lead to war.[202]

Probably even more dangerous is the growing contention between China and Japan over the uninhabited islands known as the Senkaku chain in Japan and the Diaoyu chain in China. This island chain northeast of Taiwan is close to key shipping lanes and rich fishing grounds, and it is also thought that there may be large oil reserves in the area. Rising Japanese imperialism grabbed these islands in 1895 along with Okinawa and Taiwan, but now rising Chinese imperialism demands them. There have been both Chinese and Japanese ships patrolling around these islands at different times, and increasingly vociferous threats from both sides.[203] Japan has also promised help to the Philippines and other countries in their disputes with China in the South China Sea.[204]

There has also been a lot of nationalist mass belligerence in China, on the Internet and in mass demonstrations in the streets, over the Senkaku/Diaoyu islands dispute in particular.[205]

Some Chinese government newspapers have even questioned the right of Japan to control Okinawa and the rest of the Ryukyu island chain.[206] Hundreds of years ago this island chain did have a long established "tributary relationship" with China. Will China someday go so far as to demand that all the lands over which the old Chinese Emperor once had a tributary relationship should actually still today be part of China?! This would include Mongolia, Vietnam, Korea—and perhaps even Japan itself! Well, it is unlikely that even the new Chinese imperialists will ever claim that much![207] Like other imperialists they have generally adjusted to the need for neocolonialism, rather than outright colonies or incorporation into China itself—at least with regard to other major Asian countries. It is a different matter with regard to reefs or small islands, however.

There have also been some recent border incidents between China and India, which suggest a somewhat more aggressive policy by China in that region. India provoked an outright border war with China in 1962, which it lost, and was forced to remove its "Forward Policy" military bases from the Chinese side of the de facto border. Despite minor incidents from time to time, things were mostly stable along that border until 2009 when there was a new (but quite limited) flair up. It is not known to us for sure which side was responsible for that incident, but the underlying motivation is clear (as one observer commented):

> "Since 2006, Chinese strategic experts, bloggers, retired diplomats and think tanks linked to the People's Liberation Army have been discussing the possibility of a 'partial border war' to 'teach India a lesson.' Parallels are being drawn to the pre-1962 situation, when Beijing blamed India for Tibetan uprising and New Delhi provoked China with its 'Forward Policy' on the border. China has referred to India's current troop movements as a 'New Forward Policy.' The Indian media, always wary of China, have chimed in by sensationalizing alleged border incursions and by hyping 'the China threat.' India's military has bolstered its presence in areas bordering Tibet. The military forces of both sides are once again pushing into remote and previously (for the most part) unoccupied mountainous frontier regions.
>
> "Adding fuel to this fire is mounting confidence on the Chinese side that China would win any conflict and reap broader strategic rewards from doing so. PLA generals believe India's military remains inferior in combat, logistics and war-fighting capability. Should the PLA succeed in occupying Tawang, a town near the border, and giving India's military a bloody nose, the Chinese thinking goes, Indian leaders would be much more deferential in dealing with China. A short and swift victory would underscore the need for other countries in Asia, especially U.S. friends and allies, to accommodate China's growing power by aligning with, rather than against, Beijing."[208]

Frankly, there now appears to us to be growing imperialist/expansionist thinking on both sides of the Sino-Indian border!

Back in 1979 China, which was already controlled by Deng Xiaoping and his fellow capitalist-roaders, followed through on such a threat to teach another country "a lesson" via military attack. The Sino-Vietnamese War was initiated by China for geopolitical reasons. It was presented at the time as an effort to force Vietnam out of its recent invasion of Cambodia. But it was actually more about whether China or the Soviet-backed regime in Vietnam would have suzerainty over Cambodia and Laos. I.e., it was about competing imperialist spheres of control. As Henry Kissinger, that notorious American master of "realpolitik" put it, "Whatever the shortcomings of its execution, the Chinese campaign reflected a serious, long-term strategic analysis."[209]

There was another incident along the Sino-Indian border in April 2013, but it was very minor. A platoon of Chinese soldiers ventured 20 km inside what the Indian side considered the previous line of control and refused to leave for three weeks.[210] Tensions rose, but then both sides backed off.

However, much greater contention between China and India is developing because of China's naval expansion into the Indian Ocean. Since 2008 the Chinese PLA Navy has sent at least 10 missions to "fight piracy off of Somalia".[211] More significantly, however, there has been a rapid expansion of Chinese submarine activity in the Indian Ocean, according to the Indian Navy.

A Chinese submarine operating in the Indian Ocean[212]

During the Mao era, when China was a genuinely socialist country, there was very strong opposition to imperialism and against imperialist operations in Asia especially. Revolutionary China went so far as to risk its own survival by directly supporting Korea in the Korean War, and by helping Vietnam on a tremendous scale during the U.S. imperialist war against Vietnam. In both wars the U.S. seriously considered attacking China with nuclear weapons! These anti-imperialist actions were carried out by China on the basis of proletarian internationalism.

Today, however, China's actions in the international arena are done entirely on the basis of what is in the interests of the Chinese capitalist-imperialist ruling class. Bourgeois nationalism has completely replaced proletarian internationalism.

22. Inter-imperialist contention between the U.S. and China.

It is true that the United States is trying to surround China and "contain it". It is true that the U.S. is seeking to strengthen its allies which surround China—including Japan and India—and further encourage their already strong inclinations to expand their own military strength and more strongly contest China's economic and military penetration of their areas.*

* However, it should also be kept in mind that there are plenty of contradictions between the U.S. and Japan and even more so between the U.S. and India! For one discussion of this see "So near, and yet...: America and India remain so far apart on so many issues", Banyan column, *Economist*, June 29, 2013, p. 40. And while the U.S. is encouraging Japan's military growth, it is also highly critical of Japan's growing glorification of its imperial wars in the 1930s and during World War II! [See: "The U.S. Needs to Rebuke a Japanese Ally", *Bloomberg Businessweek*, Feb. 24–March 2, 2014, p. 8.]

What we have here is a familiar scenario of a rising imperialist power trying to break out of its original restricted sphere, and a reaction by existing imperialist (and sub-imperialist or expansionist) powers to try to prevent or contain this rising new competitor. The same thing happened with the rise of Germany in Europe first in the late 19th century and then again in the mid-20th century, with the rise of Japan in the Pacific in the 20th century, and with the rise of Soviet social-imperialism in the second half of the 20th century. The world has seen this situation before!

Inter-imperialist contention is inevitable, economically, ideologically, politically and militarily. The growing belligerence of China, and the corresponding growth in re-energized arrogance in the U.S., Japan and India, and other countries, is simply an illustration of imperialist logic at work in the world today.

And this inter-imperialist contention and belligerence, between China and the U.S. and its allies, will inevitably get much worse over time.

An interesting question to consider is why this contention and hostility between China and the U.S. "bloc" has not *already* become qualitatively worse! One reason for this is that the U.S. was focused for more than a decade on its so-called "War on Terror" as the primary means of recasting its military alliances (which were originally set up as part of the anti-Soviet Cold War struggle).

A neoconservative movement began festering within the U.S. ruling class in the 1990s, after the collapse of the U.S.S.R. This exemplified a rising new belligerence within the U.S. bourgeoisie, and a feeling of "triumphalism" after the collapse of their arch-enemy, the social-imperialist Soviet Union. These "neocons" called for wars in the Middle East, including a war to replace Saddam Hussein in Iraq with a more compliant U.S. puppet. And they also called for a much more confrontational policy towards China and much stronger military support for the Taiwan regime.[213]

When the new George W. Bush Administration first came to power in early 2001 this neoconservative belligerence came to power with him. They already recognized rising China as a serious new worry for the existing world imperialist system led by the U.S. (and which they wanted to see dominated *much more* by the U.S.!) This new administration quite clearly aimed to sound the alarm of a new "Cold War" challenge from China. A May 2001 report in *Newsweek* stated:

> "The main target of the new doctrine is Beijing, not Moscow. A core group of administration officials—led by Rumsfeld's deputy Paul Wolfowitz—believes that now is the time to raise the American military profile in Asia while China is still too weak to respond. Or, as one senior administration official put it, 'China is not yet a great power but is clearly going to be.'"[214]

But then the 9/11 al Qaeda attack occurred in New York City and Washington, D.C. The U.S. ruling class—ever opportunistic!—seized upon this horrific but rather isolated event to launch imperialist wars in Afghanistan and Iraq, and more generally its international open-ended "War on Terror" largely focused against Islamic countries and peoples. But this meant that the planned increased confrontation with China, and the developments toward a new Cold War with China, had to be put on hold. The neocons projected an early and easy triumph in Afghanistan and Iraq, and then they could turn their attention to Iran, Syria, and North Korea—and finally back to the adversary they feared as the most strategic threat over the long term, China.

However, the U.S. imperialist wars in Afghanistan and Iraq have failed for the U.S. Despite the massive military efforts and the expenditure of many trillions of dollars, the wars have dragged on and on, for well over a decade already. (Officially the U.S. war in Iraq was finally declared over in late 2011, but the insurrection continues and the situation is very unstable and has been heating up again recently. And many U.S. troops remain in the region.) And the unity of the "coalition forces", in both funding the wars and providing troops, has gone from unstable to having serious and widening cracks.

This U.S. preoccupation with Afghanistan and the Middle East has given Chinese imperialism a major breathing space to expand its economic penetration of the world within the framework of the current world imperialist system, and with only limited and often clumsy U.S.

efforts to obstruct or slow down this Chinese expansion. Witness China's winning of the largest Iraq oil contracts after years of the U.S.-led war!

However, in the background there has been a growing alarm within U.S. ruling class think tanks and ideological circles about this rapid Chinese advance. They see in almost a panic that China will replace them quite soon as the largest economy in the world. They see China's international financial resources and strength grow by leaps and bounds while their own financial situation and government budget deficits become ever more serious. They watch in a cold sweat as China rapidly expands its military spending and strength, year after year. China is rising and the U.S. is declining in an overall way, and the U.S. ruling class is desperately worried about this continuing trend.

The U.S. bourgeoisie has generally recognized by now that it has to take some major actions to try to reverse this present international trend running against them. They know they need to wind down their current unaffordable wars in the Middle East and Afghanistan—though this is proving very difficult for them to do. They know they need to seek ways to outflank China in their international economic struggle.

One such economic effort at present is the so-called "Trans-Pacific Partnership" (TPP), which is a free trade zone they are pushing for the U.S.* and all the other countries on the Pacific Rim *except for China!* (I.e., China is the obvious target here.) [215] This is an example of how the U.S., *as well as China,* is now engaging in policies which will likely eventually lead to the realignment of countries and the formation of two contending economic/political/military blocs within the world imperialist system (and maybe even eventually into two more or less separate imperialist alliances!).

There is also growing U.S. and other international economic struggle against China *within* the WTO.[216] *All* the major imperialist pow-

* However, the Obama Administration is having a very difficult time getting this agreement OK'd even by its own Congress—which in this period of growing economic and political difficulties for the U.S. is more divided than ever! ["American Trade Policy", *Economist,* Feb. 22, 2014, p. 8.]

ers which are part of the WTO actually violate its rules and cheat on a regular basis (e.g., through "dumping"—selling goods in foreign markets at below cost in order to steal market share; via the use of export subsidies; promising military aid in exchange for contracts granted to its own corporations; illegal techniques such as bribery; and many other such methods). And this is especially true of the U.S. Consequently the huge difficultly for the U.S., Europe and others in trying to penalize China for such transgressions is that China is an expert at playing tit-for-tat; it invariably turns around and invokes WTO rules against similar transgressions by its accusers! This has made the U.S. in particular somewhat "gun shy" about trying to invoke WTO rules against China. And this explains in part why the bigger thrust of U.S. economic struggle against China now takes the form of attempting to create free trade associations with other countries but excluding China.

But while the U.S. is working to set up free trade zones excluding China, China in turn is fighting back in various ways. It is considering attempting to join the TPP if the U.S. is unable to stop it from doing so (and because it probably feels it will win out within that organization's rules and requirements just as it has already been winning out within the rules of the WTO). And secondly, China is—in the same fashion as the U.S.—working to set up its own free trade associations that exclude its primary opponent! For example it is promoting its own free trade zone with the ASEAN group of countries.[217]

Similarly, China is seeking to set up some other economic/political/military alliances in opposition to the U.S. and its close allies. One important effort in this direction is the Shanghai Cooperation Organization with China and Russia at its core, but also involving other countries including a number in central Asia.* Related to this

---

* The Shanghai Cooperation Organization (SCO) was formed in 1996, and now has six full members. It has military as well as political and economic aspects to it. In 2006 the Russian Foreign Minister claimed that increased threats of "terrorism, extremism and separation" made necessary increased coordination of the armed forces of the SCO member states. In 2005, 2007 and 2009 China and Russia teamed up for large-scale war games. [See: http://www.cfr.org/china/shanghai-cooperation-organization/p10883] At the 2007 SCO summit (years before the BRICS Development Bank was launched in 2013), the Iranian Vice President said

is a very recent proposal by China to set up a new "Silk Road Free Trade Zone" including China and the central Asian countries of Kazakhstan, Uzbekistan, Turkmenistan, Kyrgyzstan, and Tajikistan. In addition, this central Asian free trade zone may possibly include Afghanistan, Pakistan and even Iran![218]

Economic struggle between the U.S. and China takes many other forms as well. The U.S., for example, frequently blocks or tries to block moves by Chinese corporations to buy companies in the U.S. (and sometimes companies in other countries too) using mostly phony excuses such as "national security". But China has many ways of harming U.S. economic interests in turn.

Recently, for example, China has started cracking down on U.S. and other foreign corporations (especially pharmaceutical giants) operating in China for engaging in bribery and other illegal activities.[219] Somewhat humorously, western apologists for these companies have defended them by claiming that "this is the way things are done in China", and that it is "unfair" for the Chinese government to only crack down on foreign corporations for doing what all big companies have to do there! There might even be some truth to that charge, since corruption in China is very widespread. But even if there is, it only shows yet another way that the Chinese ruling class has of favoring its own locally based corporations and harming the economic interests of foreign countries.

"Playing fair" is not something that any imperialist country does when it doesn't have to! And in response in part to what seems to be the growth of Chinese "discrimination" against foreign corporations, the *Economist* magazine has been pushing what it calls its "Sinodependency index", to warn Western investors about the various vulnerabilities of American corporations especially, which may depend "too much" on profits from their operations in China.[220]

---

that the SCO "is a good venue for designing a new banking system which is independent from international banking systems." [*Mehr News Agency,* Oct. 31, 2008.] In 2009 China announced plans to provide $10 billion in loans to SCO member states to shore up their economies during the global financial crisis. These things suggest that even if the BRICS alliance itself fails, there are other possibilities for setting up alternative institutions to the IMF and World Bank.

And China does have a huge economic clout internationally, and with regard to the U.S. in particular. Because China is so important in funding U.S. fiscal and trade deficits, in many respects China has the upper hand when it comes to economic struggle between the two countries. This conditions or limits the U.S. freedom to attack or restrict China.

Still, economic, political and military contention between the two imperialist powers is definitely growing.

President Obama made the U.S. ruling class necessity to shift its geopolitical focus very clear near the end of 2011 when he announced the U.S. "rebalancing" effort, or "pivot", to Asia and the Pacific.[221] Part of what this geographic "pivot" involves is shifting more U.S. military forces out of the Middle East and Afghanistan and repositioning them in the Pacific around China. In June 2012 Leon Panetta, then U.S. Secretary of Defense, said that by 2020 about 60% of U.S. combat ships would be deployed off of Asia (up from about 50% already).[222] And as part of this pivot there has already been the deployment of additional U.S. military forces in Australia and Singapore, for example. While Obama claims this overall redeployment of forces, which has only just gotten underway, is not directed at China, anybody with any sense knows better.[223]

What we are really talking about here is the serious launching—after a long delay, and still slowly at first—of a new "Cold War" type rivalry, this time directed at China.

Of course the Chinese ruling class recognizes this full well. But they are confident because they know that their country's economic and military power vis-à-vis the U.S. is rising rapidly.

The way the Chinese bourgeoisie portrays the world situation since the collapse of the Soviet Union is that there has been a "unipolar world" which has been dominated by the United States. But they promote their challenge to the dominant hegemonic position of the U.S. as part of creating a "multipolar world".

However, from our perspective of the current existence of a single world imperialist system this could also be put differently: What has been a multipolar world dominated by this single *world imperialist system* (albeit with the U.S. as its biggest individual hegemonic power and exploiter) may well be starting to developing into more of a *bipolar world* with strong tendencies for this world imperialist system to split in two—with one part led or dominated by the U.S., and the other part led or dominated by China.

The Chinese leaders seem to tacitly agree with this; they have recently begun referring to China as the world's "second superpower".[224] American observers too are taking more and more note of China's rising clout: "China has a lot more power militarily, diplomatically and economically than it did in the past and it can tell countries like the U.K. and U.S. to back off in a way it couldn't before," says Perry Link, a professor at the University of California Riverside and well-known establishment expert on China.[225]

How does the ruling Chinese bourgeoisie itself express its central goal in the world?

Xi Jinping, China's new President and leader of the (so-called) Chinese Communist Party, is now frequently referring to what he calls the "Chinese dream". But by this he means not primarily aspirations for individual wealth, but rather for the further revival of a powerful Chinese nation (which in turn promotes great private wealth). Xi has explicitly said that this Chinese dream includes both a "dream of a strong nation" and a "dream of a strong army".[226] "He is falling back on nationalism, talking about making China the No. 1 superpower in the world," said Zhang Lifan, a Communist Party historian with ties to the leadership.[227]

23. Nationalist motives for holding the view that China cannot be an imperialist country.

A person connected with the Chinese Academy of Social Sciences attended the Left Forum in New York City in June 2013. When asked if she agreed that in light of its present export of billions of dollars of capital China is now an imperialist country she responded that China can't be imperialist because its foreign investments are not preceded and protected by military force.

This is once again a failure to understand that there is an *imperialist system*, of which China is now an integral part. China's investments around the world are in fact "preceded and protected by military force", even if—at present—that force is not yet being wielded to a significant degree by the Chinese bourgeoisie itself. According to this woman's logic Japan and Germany are not imperialist powers either, since most of the military force being used to maintain the imperialist system is currently being supplied and/or directed by the U.S. together with a few close allies.

There is in fact a tremendous reluctance even among many people who recognize full well that China is now a *capitalist* country to grant that it is also now an *imperialist* country. And this is true even among many Maoists both internationally and within China itself. What lies behind this unwillingness to recognize the obvious?

In part this is no doubt due to a failure to fully comprehend the term 'imperialism' in the Leninist sense. But it seems to us that there is a deeper cause as well; a lingering feeling among even many Chinese revolutionaries that no matter what China does today it can still only be the *victim* of foreign imperialism.

China was in fact a long and major victim of foreign imperialism (especially British, Tsarist Russian, U.S. and Japanese imperialism) for well over a century before 1949. Even after the 1949 Revolution China had to ward off U.S. imperialism in Korea (1950–1953) and help in a major way to defeat both French and U.S. imperialism in Indo-China (1949–1975). It also had to stand strong against Soviet social-imperialism and its serious military threat against China, while that existed. The feeling that China has long been the victim of foreign imperialism, and further threatened by it, is deeply ingrained in the psyche of progressive Chinese people, and rightly so.

But the bitter experience of these great historical wounds could be blinding people, including within China, to the realities of the present-day Chinese regime. Even the egregious sins of the current bourgeois ruling class in China, both against the Chinese masses and in their penetrations into foreign countries, are often blamed more on U.S. imperialism and its "manipulation" of the Chinese rulers, than on those rulers themselves. The assumption or dogma is that the Chinese ruling class is still a comprador bourgeoisie, largely under the thumb of foreign imperialism, rather than a bureaucratic national bourgeoisie promoting its own class interests against the interests of the people of China and of the whole world.

This misconception, even among many present-day Chinese followers of Mao, is a serious political error. You can't make a revolution if you don't understand the real situation you are in. If Chinese revolutionaries are unable to see that China has become an imperialist country then they are in danger of apologizing on a nationalist basis for a regime that they say they want to overthrow!

Recently many Chinese enthusiasts for Mao and the socialism of the Mao period have come to understand that the so-called Communist Part of China is completely and permanently under the control of the bourgeoisie, and cannot be won back to the proletariat by appealing to its supposedly "more revolutionary cadre". Nonetheless, many people fell for the superficial pretend "Maoist" reformism of Bo Xilai, for example (see sidebar on next two pages). To make a new proletarian revolution in China, a small but growing number of genuine Maoists agree on the need to form a *new* genuinely revolutionary Communist Party, which has not been any part of the last 35 years of the revisionist and now virtually openly capitalist party. (Thinking that Chinese society can be changed by "recapturing" the CCP is simply a naïve reformist notion, similar to the thinking that American society can be changed in some significant way by revolutionaries "capturing" the Democratic Party. It is time to reject such ideas totally.)

This is only one aspect of a new Chinese revolutionary movement as it comes to more deeply understand the nature of the political system they are up against. This nascent Chinese revolutionary movement is now insisting that China today is not a socialist country and has not been for many decades. And they are now insisting, amid growing debate, that the nature of the class struggle in China is between a ruling bureaucratic national capitalist-imperialist bourgeoisie and the alliance of the now huge proletariat and the peasantry and their allies. China is now an imperialist country, and it requires a revolutionary internationalist conception and program of opposition to Chinese imperialism. And they are rejecting the simplistic and ahistorical notion that becoming a Maoist revolutionary today means returning to the same ideas, program and strategy of opposition to foreign imperialism, the comprador bourgeoisie and the landlord class that were appropriate back in the 1930s and 1940s. Times have changed! There is a lot of work for Maoist revolutionaries to do in China and internationally to get our movement progressing on the right path!

Many Maoists and supporters of Mao outside of China have also had tendencies to fail to see that China has qualitatively changed into a capitalist-imperialist country. There are a great many people around

Bo Xilai was a powerful leader of the CCP and member of the Politburo who was forced from power after his wife, Gu Kailai, was charged with murdering a British businessman, and Bo was said to have obstructed her prosecution. After Bo's fall she was arrested and convicted. Bo was charged with bribery, graft, improper sexual relations with several women and abuse of power. Like nearly all Chinese leaders today, he and his family have become enormously rich—and this was not from their modest official salaries! His trial began on Aug. 22, 2013, and he was convicted a few weeks later and sentenced to life imprisonment. ["Bo Xilai Set to Face Trial This Week as Historic Case Nears End", *Bloomberg News*, Aug. 18, 2013, online at: http://www.bloomberg.com/news/2013-08-18/bo-xilai-trial-set-for-aug-22-in-jinan-xinhua-says.html]

Bo is what is known as a "Princeling", i.e. one of the descendants of the most powerful revisionist leaders of the CCP who have become sort of a hereditary nobility in China. (His father was Bo Yibo, one of the so-called "eight immortals" of the CCP, who—led by Deng Xiaoping—destroyed socialism and restored capitalism in China.) As the Party leader of the city of Chongqing, Bo Xilai tried to build a personal power base for his career by cracking down on rampant organized crime, promoting some welfare

the world who have been part of the anti-imperialist and revolutionary movements and who have spent many years defending revolutionary China against scurrilous attacks and lies. Naturally we have developed a deep appreciation for Mao and the Chinese Revolution. But today's China is no longer that Maoist revolutionary China which drew our strong affection and support, and our ideas must correspondingly change as well. While continuing to uphold Mao and the Maoist era in China, and the world-shaking Great Proletarian Cultural Revolution, we can no longer in good conscience uphold or support the capitalist-imperialist country that China has now become. Our allegiance is not with China, but with the revolutionary people's struggle, in China and around the world.

programs, and appealing to mass nostalgia for the socialism of the Mao years. He even encouraged some superficial Maoist trappings such as waving red flags and the singing of old revolutionary songs. He tried to "ride the tide" of growing rebellion and new revolutionary sentiment, but also, according to some reports, betrayed revolutionary comrades at a critical juncture, in order to save his own skin from government attack. As we've seen, he failed. But his political and economic program was as solidly capitalist as any other contemporary leader the CCP. It is doubtful if he was any more corrupt than any of the other present CCP leaders. However, his "Maoist public image" and campaigning for mass support alarmed many other leaders of the Party, and they took the opportunity which presented itself when the murder which his wife committed came to light, as well as Bo Xilai's own purported role in attempting to cover it up, to remove him from power.

At best Bo was merely a bourgeois reformist and not a Maoist revolutionary; at worst he was a corrupt populist demagogue. We're not sure which. There is an important general moral here: People need to be alert to the possible existence of reformist populists who fool the masses into thinking that they are revolutionaries.

24. Summation: Some general theses.

1. The present era is the monopoly capitalist or imperialist stage of capitalism. Imperialism, in the modern sense, is capitalist-imperialism, the modern stage of capitalism.

2. All capitalist ruling classes in this era function within the world imperialist system and seize all of the world's wealth and resources they are able to. However:

   a. The bourgeoisie (including its alliance in some cases with a feudal landlord class) *in most countries* is far too weak internationally to exercise significant imperialist control over other countries, or to organize significant economic exploitation of them.

   b. In a few countries the ruling bourgeoisie is far stronger, and has quite a free hand to boss around other countries and/or to economically exploit them to a considerable degree. These are the countries we call *imperialist countries.*

3. After World War II world imperialism underwent some major changes. One of these very important changes was the forced replacement (in part because of people's rebellions) of most outright colonies which had been under the exclusive control of a single imperialist power with *neocolonialism.* Under this new arrangement, most countries in Africa, Latin America, the Middle East and Asia are now officially independent of their former colonial masters, but are still subject to foreign imperialist exploitation and political or military interference.

4. An aspect of neocolonialism that still often goes underappreciated is that the neocolonies are now open to imperialist predation *by more than one* imperialist power, and actually by *all* imperialist powers at the present time.

5. This change to neocolonialism and the exploitation of neocolonies by *all* the major imperialist countries required the construction of an *imperialist system* to regulate this joint exploitation of the world,

and to create and/or impose rules for how these vicious wolves would prey on the sheep, without constantly coming into bloody conflict against each other. International agencies, such as the IMF, the World Bank, and the World Trade Organization were set up to regulate this new imperialist system.

6. Imperialism, even more so than capitalism in general, requires a strong military force to maintain it. The world imperialist system is also maintained by imperialist invasions and wars, when "necessary". There are nearly always one or more such imperialist wars in progress.

7. However, in contrast to the successes in setting up international *economic* organizations to regulate the world imperialist system, there have been much greater difficulties in trying to establish a fully functional *international military force* to keep the world imperialist system together. The contradictions between imperialist powers have prevented the U.N. from assuming that role, and U.N. "peace keeping" forces can only be used where all the Security Council members are in full agreement. NATO and similar military alliances also do not represent *all* the current imperialist powers, and there are contradictions within even NATO which prevents its employment in some cases. This inability to create a central military force to control the world imperialist system is further reason to conclude that this system is not at all the same as "ultra-imperialism" of the sort Kautsky envisioned.

8. Thus since World War II the primary "world policeman" in the Western imperialist bloc, and now in the world imperialist system, has been the United States. This is, in a way, an adaptation in the new neocolonial circumstances, of the requirement in the colonial era in which each imperialist power had to maintain political and military control of its own colonies by means of its own military establishment.

9. Because of its initial overwhelming advantage in military and economic might at the end of World War II, the U.S. obtained special benefits and privileges within this world imperialist system.

10. However, *all* the major capitalist powers which were part of the Western bloc, or are now part of the world imperialist system, have a generally free hand (both formally and practically) to economically exploit the countries which the U.S. military (often with the very significant participation of other powers) keeps open for exploitation.

11. This new imperialist system which was organized at the end of World War II did not at first cover the entire world. The socialist Soviet Union and its allies in Eastern Europe were outside this imperialist system. And in 1949 the Chinese Revolution also removed China from the developing imperialist system.

12. When the once socialist Soviet Union was captured by a newly arisen bourgeois state-capitalist class centered in the CPSU itself, it also soon became a new imperialist power. From that time on there were then *two* largely independent imperialist systems in the world, the Western imperialist bloc and the Soviet social-imperialist bloc.

13. While Mao was still alive China was then the only major region of the world which remained outside the two imperialist spheres of control. And this was only possible to maintain even in China because of the vitally important Great Proletarian Cultural Revolution which began in 1966, initiated and led by Mao.

14. When the state-capitalist Soviet Union finally collapsed completely in 1989–1991, the Soviet social-imperialist bloc collapsed along with it. Russia and the other countries in this bloc shifted unevenly and to varying degrees into the other imperialist bloc, which became a single world imperialist system. Russia has had only extremely limited success in trying to at least keep the internal nations of the old Soviet Union together as a sort of bloc within the world imperialist system, much less in extending its influence beyond it.

15. After Mao's death in 1976 a rising new bourgeoisie within the CCP, and led by the notorious capitalist-roader and traitor to the proletariat Deng Xiaoping, seized control of the Party and the state.

16. Though originally exclusively a state-capitalist bourgeoisie, this new Chinese ruling class decided to move to a considerable degree toward the Western private monopoly capitalist model. This it called a "reform", and an "opening up" to foreign investment and joining the world capitalist market.

17. As the economic transformation of China from socialism back to capitalism was completed, China began to show some early signs of its rising new imperialist nature. It began to export capital, and then greatly expanded this, finding special opportunities in the "vacuum" in Africa (which the established imperialist countries had been largely ignoring) and in Latin America and even Europe, in part because of the international financial crisis, thus taking advantage of the weaknesses of the other imperialist powers. And China began working feverishly to expand its military might for the eventual purpose of protecting and expanding its ever-growing foreign economic assets.

18. In the new millennium China's imperialist export of capital has been multiplying extremely rapidly, and China is also beginning to demonstrate its rapidly growing political and military might. With its announced program of "going out" it has now arrived as a fully fledged new imperialist power.

19. Since the 1949 proletarian revolution in China, the ruling class in China (originally representing the proletariat, but since the coup after Mao's death a new ruling class representing the bureaucratic national bourgeoisie centered in the CCP itself) has been largely politically independent of foreign imperialist controls.

20. The uneven development of capitalism and imperialism has already led to the very noticeable relative decline of the U.S., Japan and Europe, while Chinese economic, political and military power has been expanding rapidly.

21. In addition, the still-developing world overproduction crisis has already harmed the U.S., Japan and Europe quite seriously. While China too has been somewhat harmed by the world eco-

nomic crisis, this has been much less so than elsewhere because of China's much greater ability to further expand government and consumer debt. This difference will very likely continue at least for some time.

22. Thus, on the world imperialist scene, China is continuing to rise and grow stronger, while the U.S. and its allies are in decline. This is leading toward intensified inter-imperialist economic, political and military contention.

23. Even the present world imperialist system itself appears to have a serious division developing within it. It may well be once again starting to divide into two semi-independent and contending/conflicting imperialist blocs.

24. Capitalist-imperialism is a system filled with serious and ever-worsening internal problems and contradictions. But many view world imperialism as being all-powerful and destined to last forever. Similarly, it is difficult for many to see other imperialist powers grow into serious challengers or opponents of U.S. domination *within* the world imperialist system. But the crises and contradictions of the system, which have especially surfaced in the last decade, reveal even deeper crises and the vulnerabilities of the U.S.'s domination and of the world system as a whole. The same vulnerabilities which lead to inter-imperialist rivalries and blocs, also lead to the very real possibilities of revolution in countries around the world, including inside imperialist countries themselves!

25. A huge and continuing obstacle to the growth of revolutionary forces is the problem that many of these developing forces narrow their horizons and get caught up in turning their opposition to one imperialist power into support for another. While the twisted path toward revolution always requires tactical flexibility and temporary alliances, it is essential for revolutionary forces to never adopt "main danger" *strategies*, or choosing the "lesser of two evils", which downplay or make optional the independence of revolutionary forces. Many times, once-revolutionary forces have become mere appendages to one side or the other in (direct or proxy) inter-imperialist

struggles—and have even attempted to join the system, against its challengers. It is vitally important to maintain our revolutionary political independence.

26. For many, internationalism is just a slogan, an educational mission punctuated by occasional solidarity demonstrations. But revolutionary internationalists place a high priority on *internationalist* communist work to spur the development of joint and fraternal internationalist campaigns among the proletariat and revolutionary people, across borders and worldwide, in defiance of imperialist and proxy-imperialist divisions, with special defiance of racism and xenophobia. For this reason, internationalism is essential in building the revolutionary forces to bring imperialism—the entire world imperialist system—to an end, and to begin the work of a new world.

27. For the working people and poor of the world the hope of the future is not to be found in either of the two developing imperialist blocs, or in vainly attempting to support one of them against the other. On the contrary, our task is to build an international revolutionary force in all lands to overthrow the world capitalist-imperialist system as a whole! World imperialism is in growing crisis and ever more serious disarray, and the material conditions for world revolution are developing rapidly. Let us imbue the masses with the revolutionary spirit necessary to free the world from the perpetual horrors of capitalist-imperialism!

*Appendix: Exposing and Refuting Kautsky and his Opportunist Theory of "Ultra-Imperialism"**

"ULTRA-IMPERIALISM" — AN OPPORTUNIST THEORY IN THE SERVICE OF MONOPOLY CAPITAL

Lenin exploded the falsity of the theory of "ultraimperialism" advanced by Kautsky. He regarded it as the most subtle of opportunist theories, most skillfully counterfeited to appear scientific.

Kautsky asked:

> Cannot the present imperialist policy be supplanted by a new, ultra-imperialist policy, which will introduce the joint exploitation of the world by internationally united finance capital in place of the mutual rivalries of national finance capitals? (Quoted by Lenin in "Imperialism, the Highest Stage of Capitalism", op. *ext.,* p. 293)

He went on to say that the end of the war:

> "may lead to the strengthening of the weak rudiments of ultraimperialism. ... Its lessons may hasten developments for which we would have to wait a long time under peace conditions. If an agreement between nations, disarmament and a lasting peace are achieved, the worst of the causes that led to the growing moral decay of capitalism before the war may disappear. . . ." (Quoted by Lenin in "The Collapse of the Second International", op. *ext.,* p. 184) He said that this "new" phase of "ultra-imperialism" "could create an era of new hopes and expectations within the framework of capitalism". (*ibid.,* p. 185)

* From *Lenin's Fight Against Revisionism and Opportunism,* by Cheng Yen-Shih, (Foreign Languages Press, Peking, 1965), Chapter 9. Exposing and Refuting Kautskyism.

With his theory of "ultra-imperialism" Kautsky wanted to prove that the contradictions of capitalism would be greatly mitigated. Lenin pointed out that free trade and peaceful competition were possible and necessary during the former "peaceful" epoch of capitalism, when capital was in a position to increase the number of its colonies and dependent countries without hindrance, and when concentration of capital was still slight and no monopolist undertakings existed. However, in the imperialist epoch, though monopoly superseded free competition it did not abolish competition; on the contrary, it intensified it, thus compelling the capitalists to pass from peaceful expansion to armed struggle for the redivision of colonies and spheres of influence.

Lenin said:

> The capitalists divide the world, not out of any particular malice, but because the degree of concentration which has been reached forces them to adopt this method in order to obtain profits. And they divide it "in proportion to capital", "in proportion to strength", because there cannot be any other method of division under commodity production and capitalism. But strength varies with the degree of economic and political development. In order to understand what is taking place, it is necessary to know what questions are settled by the changes in strength. The question as to whether these changes are "purely" economic or non-economic (e.g., military) is a secondary one, which cannot in the least affect fundamental views on the latest epoch of capitalism. ("Imperialism, the Highest Stage of Capitalism", *op. ext.,* p. 253)

He added:

> ... "inter-imperialist" or "ultra-imperialist" alliances, no matter what form they may assume, whether of one imperialist coalition against another, or of a general alliance embracing *all* the imperialist powers, are *inevitably* nothing more than a "truce" in periods between wars. Peaceful al-

> liances prepare the ground for wars, and in their turn grow out of wars; the one conditions the other, producing alternating forms of peaceful and non-peaceful struggle on *one and the same* basis of imperialist connections and relations within world economics and world politics. (*ibid.*, p. 295)

The only real, social significance which Kautsky's "ultra-imperialism" could have was that

> "it is a most reactionary method of consoling the masses with hopes of permanent peace being possible under capitalism, by distracting their attention from the sharp antagonisms and acute problems of the present times, and directing it towards illusory prospects of an imaginary 'ultraimperialism' of the future". (*ibid.*, p. 294)

Kautsky played the part of the parson saying that many capitalists were urgently interested in universal peace and disarmament, and were not bound to imperialism, because any interests they might gain from war and armaments did not outweigh the damage they might suffer from the consequences. He advised the capitalists that the urge of capital to expand could be best promoted, "not by the violent methods of imperialism, but by peaceful democracy". (Quoted by Lenin in "Imperialism, the Highest Stage of Capitalism", *ibid.*, p. 289) Lenin remarked:

> And now that the armed conflict for Great Power privileges is a fact, Kautsky tries to *persuade* the capitalists and the petty bourgeoisie to believe that war is a terrible thing, while disarmament is a good thing, in exactly the same way, and with exactly the same results, as a Christian parson tries from the pulpit to persuade the capitalist to believe that human love is God's commandment, as well as the yearning of the soul and the moral law of civilisation. The thing that Kautsky calls economic tendencies towards "ultra-imperialism" is precisely a petty-bourgeois attempt to *persuade* the financiers to refrain from doing evil. ("The Collapse of the Second International", *op. cit.*, p. 190)

He showed that, as an international ideological trend, Kautskyism was both a product of the disintegration and decay of the Second International, and at the same time an inevitable outcrop of the ideology of the petty bourgeoisie who remained captive to bourgeois prejudices.

He declared:

> The growing world proletarian revolutionary movement in general, and the communist movement in particular, cannot dispense with an analysis and exposure of the theoretical errors of Kautskyism. The more so since pacifism and "democracy" in general, which lay no claim to Marxism whatever, but which, like Kautsky and Co., are obscuring the profundity of the contradictions of imperialism and the inevitable revolutionary crisis to which it gives rise, are still very widespread all over the world. ("Imperialism, the Highest Stage of Capitalism", *op. cit.*, pp. 192–93)

NOTES

1. V. I. Lenin, "Imperialism, the Highest Stage of Capitalism: A Popular Outline", (Peking: Foreign Languages Press, 1975 (1916)), p. 106. Online in a slightly different translation from *Lenin's Selected Works*, vol. 1, (Moscow: 1963), at: http://www.marxists.org/archive/lenin/works/1916/imp-hsc/

2. Ibid., p. 105.

3. Scott H., "Lenin on Imperialism" (circa 2007), online at http://www.massline.org/PolitEcon/ScottH/LeninOnImperialism.pdf

4. Samir Amin, "Imperialism and Globalization", *Monthly Review*, Vol. 53, #2, June 2001, p. 6. See also the link in the note above for further criticism of Amin's conception of imperialism.

5. See for example, Samir Amin, "China 2013", *Monthly Review*, Vol. 64, #10, March 2013, online at: http://monthlyreview.org/2013/03/01/china-2013 Amin explicitly avoids the "too abstract question" of whether China is presently socialist or capitalist, but nevertheless insists that China remains on the "socialist path" that it embarked on in 1950! He recognizes that China is an "emerging power" but refuses to think of this as meaning an imperialist power.

6. Sison wrote "It is of urgent necessity that we learn about the social, economic, political and cultural degradation that China has undergone since the start of the capitalist restoration, in the face of false claims that China has become well developed, is responsive to the people's needs, and is rising as an imperialist rival of the United States." [From his foreword to Pao-yu Ching, *Revolution and Counterrevolution: China's Continuing Class Struggle Since Liberation* (Manila: Institute of Political Economy, 2012).] Certainly it is true that the new bourgeoisie ruling China is not "responsive to the people's needs"; but it flies in the face of reality to deny that China has undergone a very rapid economic development, or to fail to see that China is now a rapidly rising imperialist power.

7. "The Communist Party of the Philippines on Maoism, New Democratic Revolution, China & the Current World", an interview with Prof. Jose Maria Sison, Founding Chairman of the Communist Party of the Philippines, by *New Culture Magazine* of the Communist Reconstruction Union of Brazil, not dated, but apparently from late 2013 or else January 2014. Online at: http://www.josemariasison.org/?p=13979 [as of Jan. 25, 2014].

8. For a brief discussion of this British-caused famine in India and further references see: http://www.massline.org/Dictionary/FA.htm#famines_imperialist

9. In 2011 Arvind Subramanian of the Peterson Institute for International Economics even predicted that "the renminbi could replace the dollar as the world's largest reserve currency" within 10 years! [Charles Kenny, "The Case for Second Place", *Bloomberg Businessweek*, Oct. 17–23, 2011, p. 15.]

10. For the increase in this percentage of cross investment up through the 1960s see: Michael Barratt Brown, "The Economics of Imperialism" (Penguin: 1974), esp. pp. 207–8. "[T]he direction of U.S. investment is not now so much to ex-colonial or under-developed lands as to other industrially developed states. This is true for all the main capital-exporting countries.... About a half of all their capital exports went to each other in the 1960s."

11. Lenin, "Imperialism, the Highest Stage of Capitalism: A Popular Outline", (Peking: Foreign Languages Press, 1975 (1916)), pp. 75–76.

12. Heriberto Araújo and Juan Pablo Cardenal, "China's Economic Empire", *New York Times*, June 1, 2013. Online at: http://www.nytimes.com/2013/06/02/opinion/sunday/chinas-economic-empire.html?nl=todaysheadlines&emc=edit_th_20130602 It is true, however, that this is a recent new trend, in part brought about by the recent aggravation of financial problems within the Euro zone.

13. "China's outward investment: The Second Wave", *Economist*, Oct. 26, 2013, pp. 72–73.

14. Richard Silk, "Investment Into China Flattens", *Wall Street Journal*, May 16, 2013, online at: http://online.wsj.com/article/SB10001424127887324767004578486181643410080.html

15. Lenin, "Imperialism, the Highest Stage of Capitalism: A Popular Outline", (Peking: Foreign Languages Press, 1975 (1916)), p. 117.

16. See "Asian Tigers" entry in the Dictionary of Revolutionary Marxism.

17. "Criticism of 'Taking the Three Directives as the Key Link'", an unsigned article criticizing Deng Xiaoping, *Peking* Review, Vol. 19, #14, April 2, 1976, available online at: http://www.massline.org/PekingReview/PR1976/PR1976-14b.htm

18. Source: World Bank, List of countries by GDP (nominal), rounded to nearest 0.1%, online at http://en.wikipedia.org/wiki/List_of_countries_by_GDP_%28nominal%29 The percentage figures for 2012 have been calculated by us from the world and national estimates for nominal GDP made by the IMF, in a table online at: http://en.wikipedia.org/wiki/World_gdp (accessed summer 2013).

19. "In the early postwar period, U.S. industrial production comprised 56.4 per cent of the capitalist world's total; its exports 23.6 per cent and its gold reserves, 71.3 per cent." —Yen Yao-chun, "The Economic Origins of U.S. Imperialist Policies of Aggression and War", *Peking Review*, #4, Jan. 27, 1961, p. 12, online at: http://www.massline.org/PekingReview/PR1961/PR1961-04.pdf

20. For a little further explanation of the PPP conversion factor, see the "Purchasing Power Parity" entry in the Dictionary of Revolutionary Marxism, online at: http://www.massline.org/Dictionary/PU.htm#purchasing_power_parity

21. Source: World Bank, top 10 countries by nominal GDP and GDP-PPP for the year 2012, rounded to nearest 0.1%, online at http://en.wikipedia.org/wiki/World_Bank_historical_list_of_ten_largest_countries_by_GDP#Highest_GDP_share_by_country_.28World_Bank_statistics.29 The percentages of world GDP-PPP for the U.S. and China were calculated by us from the country and world figures.

22. Source: The China Global Trade website at: http://www.chinaglobaltrade.com/article/us-manufacturing-and-trade-with-china

23. For a short article on the Gini coefficient with values for selected countries in specific years see the entry in the Dictionary of Revolutionary Marxism at http://www.massline.org/Dictionary/GI.htm The Gini figures in the text come from that chart.

24. The information in this paragraph about Chinese SOEs, as well as the chart, come from "China: Changing the Economy: The Long Weekend", *Economist*, Nov. 2, 2013, pp. 49–50.

25. "Businesses Enjoy Expanded Powers", *Beijing Review*, Vol. 27, #25, June 18, 1984, p. 10. Online at: http://www.massline.org/PekingReview/PR1984/PR1984-25.pdf

26. Ibid., pp. 10–11.

27. Bruce Dickson, *Red Capitalists in China* (2003), pp. 107–108.

28. Kelly Liu & Kevin Daly, "Foreign Direct Investment in China Manufacturing Industry—Transformation from a Low Tech to High Tech Manufacturing", *International Journal of Business and Management*, Vol. 6, #7, July 2011, Table 3. Online at: http://www.google.com/url?sa=t&rct=j&q=&esrc=s&source=web&cd=1&ved=0CD0QFjAA&url=http%3A%2F%2Fwww.ccsenet.org%2Fjournal%2Findex.php%2Fijbm%2Farticle%2Fdownload%2F9232%2F7900&ei=D53FUpbUI8P9oATJqICoAQ&usg=AFQjCNFtNEMkloZfQb7fV-LllztAbOss_w&sig2=viGucJ_cfij7ca8o3iSvYQ&bvm=bv.58187178,d.cGU. However, by our calculation, the percentage of foreign-funded exports in 2008 was 55.34%

(rather than 55.25% as the authors state here) if official statistics from the Chinese government are used. (See next footnote for the Chinese government statistical website.)

29. "Statistical Communiqué of the People's Republic of China on the 2012 National Economic and Social Development", National Bureau of Statistics of China, Feb. 22, 2013, Table 6. Online at: http://www.stats.gov.cn/english/NewsEvents/201302/t20130222_26962.html

30. Ibid.

31. Ken Davies, "Inward FDI in China and its Policy Context, 2012", Columbia FDI Profiles, Oct. 24, 2012, annex table 4, (p. 11). Online at: http://www.vcc.columbia.edu/files/vale/documents/Profiles_China_IFDI_24_Oct_2012_-_FINAL.pdf

32. Ibid.

33. "China: The economy: A bubble in pessimism", *Economist*, Aug. 17, 2013, p. 39.

34. "China's Big Banks: Giant Reality Check", *Economist*, Aug. 31, 2013, p. 61.

35. Ibid., p. 62. The data is as of the first quarter of 2013. Besides these 4 enormous Chinese banks, another one of the top ten banks in the world is HSBC, a world bank whose home turfs include both Hong Kong and the U.K. But this bank is dominated by the British imperialists.

36. Ibid., p. 61.

37. Carl E. Walter & Fraser J. T. Howie, *Red Capitalism: The Fragile Financial Foundation of China's Extraordinary Rise* (John Wiley & Sons (Asia), 2011), pp. 28–29.

38. "China's Big Banks: Giant Reality Check", *Economist*, Aug. 31, 2013, p. 61.

39. Ibid.

40. *Wall Street Journal*, Nov. 12, 2012; *New York Times*, Nov. 10, 2012.

41. "China's Big Banks: Giant Reality Check", *Economist*, Aug. 31, 2013, p. 61.

42. "A light touch", *Economist*, October 19, 2013, p. 11; and "Chinese banks: Open for business", in the same issue, p. 62.

43. "American Banks: Not big enough", a review of Richard Bove's book, *Guardians of Prosperity: Why American Needs Big Banks*, in the *Economist*, Jan. 11, 2014, p. 73.

44. Tsai Cheng, "Our Country is Now a Socialist Country Without Internal or External Debts", *Peking Review*, Vol. 12, #21, May 23, 1969, online at: http://www.massline.org/PekingReview/PR1969/PR1969-21-NoDebts.pdf

45. Vinod Mahanto, "How Nepal's first billionaire Binod Chaudhury is building a global empire", *Economic Times* [India], Jan. 31, 2014, online at: http://articles.economictimes.indiatimes.com/2014-01-31/news/46870463_1_nepal-wai-wai-kathmandu

46. One example where this seems to be the case is the interesting article by Patrick Bond, "The Rise of 'Sub-Imperialism'", *Counter-Punch*, Nov. 23–25, 2012, online at: http://www.counterpunch.org/2012/11/23/the-rise-of-sub-imperialism

47. Lenin, "Imperialism, the Highest Stage of Capitalism: A Popular Outline", (Peking: Foreign Languages Press, 1975 (1916)), p. 72.

48. Lenin, ibid., p. 76.

49. Lenin, ibid. p. 116.

50. For a brief summary of the decline of U.S. manufacturing in recent decades see: http://www.massline.org/Dictionary/MA.htm#manufacturing_U.S.

51. For information on the status of the effort to reform the voting shares of the IMF see "Acceptances of the Proposed Amendment of the Articles of Agreement on Reform of the Executive Board and Consents to 2010 Quota Increase" at: http://www.imf.org/external/np/sec/misc/consents.htm#a1

52. "BRICS reach deal over development bank", *Aljazeera*, March 27, 2013, online at: http://www.aljazeera.com/news/africa/2013/03/20133268641350653.html

53. David Smith, "BRICS eye infrastructure funding through new development bank", *Guardian* [U.K.], March 28, 2013, online at: http://www.guardian.co.uk/global-development/2013/mar/28/brics-countries-infrastructure-spending-development-bank

54. Daniel Twining of the German Marshall Fund, a U.S. ruling class institution, quoted on Wikipedia, at http://en.wikipedia.org/wiki/2013_BRICS_summit (as of June 23, 2013).

55. From the March 27, 2013, *Aljazeera* report mentioned in an endnote above.

56. "German Foreign Policy: No More Shirking", *Economist*, Feb. 8, 2014, pp. 49–50.

57. Ibid., p. 50.

58. This definition of FDI is taken from the Dictionary of Revolutionary Marxism, at: http://www.massline.org/Dictionary/FO.htm#FDI

59. Source: Thilo Hanemann & Daniel H. Rosen, "China's International Investment Position: An Update", April 23, 2013, on the website of the "Rhodium Group", at: http://rhg.com/notes/chinas-international-investment-position-an-update

60. "China's Net International Investment Position Hit US$2 Trillion in Mid-2011", by China Briefing, posted Oct. 25, 2011, at http://www.china-briefing.com/news/2011/10/25/chinas-net-international-investment-position-hit-us2-trillion-in-mid-2011.html#more-14422

61. Bureau of Economic Analysis report, June 25, 2013, U.S. Department of Commerce, online at: http://www.bea.gov/newsreleases/international/intinv/intinvnewsrelease.htm (as of June 28, 2013).

62. http://www.forbes.com/sites/kenrapoza/2013/01/23/is-chinas-ownership-of-u-s-debt-a-national-security-threat/

63. Ibid.

64. It is, unfortunately, hard to find reliable estimates of the *total* exported capital for most countries, though figures about the stock of outward FDI are easily available for the OECD and G-20 countries.

65. "FDI in Figures", OECD, February 2014, Table 4, online at: http://www.oecd.org/investment/statistics.htm

66. "FDI in Figures", OECD, op. cit., Table 4.

67. Source: "FDI in Figures", OECD, op. cit., Tables 2 and 4. The OECD figure of $62.4 billion for China's OFDI in 2012 may be in error. China's official figure for 2012 exceeded $77 billion. [*Economist*, "China's overseas investment", Jan. 19, 2013.] This would mean that China's OFDI stock is growing *even faster* than stated in the text!

68. As of the second quarter of 2013, when Lenovo surpassed HP. "PC sales decline 5 quarters in row", *San Francisco Chronicle*, July 12, 2013. Lenovo was only the 4th largest computer company in the world just after it purchased IBM's PC unit, so it has gained a lot of market share since then.

69. Randall Morck, Bernard Yeung, Minyuan Zhao, "Perspectives on China's Outward Foreign Direct Investment", June 2007, figure 1. Online at: http://

scholar.google.com/scholar_url?hl=en&q=http://www.researchgate.net/publication/5223340_Perspectives_on_China%27s_outward_foreign_direct_investment/file/32bfe5100cd8107544.pdf&sa=X&scisig=AAGBfm166mt8uM0u993N6BsDX8xQB5bSiQ&oi=scholarr

70. Graph of Chinese capital export targets is from "China's Overseas Investment", *Economist*, Jan. 19, 2013, online at: http://www.economist.com/news/china/21569775-expanding-scale-and-scope-chinas-outward-direct-investment-odi-lay-hee-ho

71. KPMY/Univ. of Sydney, "Demystifying Chinese Investment: China's Outbound Direct Investment in Australia", Aug. 2012, online at: http://www.kpmg.com/AU/en/IssuesAndInsights/ArticlesPublications/china-insights/Documents/demystifying-chinese-investment-2012.pdf And also, "Chinese looking to diversify Australian investments", *ABC News (Australia)*, June 12, 2013, online at: http://www.abc.net.au/news/2013-06-12/chinese-looking-to-diversify-australian-investments/4747262

72. "Canada top target for Chinese foreign investment last year", *iPolitics*, Feb. 13, 2013, online at: http://www.ipolitics.ca/2013/02/13/canada-top-target-for-chinese-foreign-investment-last-year/

73. "China Keen on Investing in Brazil Infrastructure, Manufacturing", *Wall Street Journal*, May 10, 2013, online at: http://online.wsj.com/article/BT-CO-20130510-715152.html

74. Hunt Kushner, "In Brazil's Red Corner", *Foreign Policy Association*, Dec. 31, 2012, online at: http://foreignpolicyblogs.com/2012/12/31/in-brazils-red-corner/

75. See *Wall Street Journal* article from May 10, 2013, in a previous footnote.

76. Paul Eckert, "Despite the politics, Chinese investment in U.S. grows", *Reuters*, online at: http://www.reuters.com/article/2013/06/09/us-usa-china-investment-idUSBRE95805X20130609

77. Ibid.

78. Ibid.

79. Ibid.

80. These particular acquisitions, and some others, are discussed in Garrett Bruno & Alisa Wiersema, "Where's the Money: Chinese Investments in U.S.", *ABC News*, June 7, 2013, online at: http://abcnews.go.com/Politics/money-chinese-investments-us/story?id=19347795#.UdYGhKw7v0Y

81. "Chinese Investors Pursue U.S. Property Deals", *New York Times*, June 25, 2013, online at: http://www.nytimes.com/2013/06/26/business/global/chinese-investors-pursue-us-real-estate-deals.html?nl=todaysheadlines&emc=edit_th_20130626

82. "China's outward investment: The Second Wave", *Economist*, Oct. 26, 2013, p. 72. The building is known as 1 Chase Manhattan Plaza, and was originally commissioned by David Rockefeller. The article compares the huge real estate investments that Japan made in the U.S. in the 1980s, many of which were ill-advised and money-losing ventures, with the current wave of Chinese investments, and concludes that "Chinese investors seem to be negotiating reasonable deals".

83. Chris Devonshire-Ellis, "Lenovo's Purchase of Motorola an Exercise in Buying Brands", *China Briefing*, Jan. 30, 2014, online at: http://www.china-briefing.com/news/2014/01/30/lenovos-purchase-of-motorola-an-exercise-in-buying-brands.html

84. "Lenovo CEO hopes $5 billion buys pay off", *Bloomberg News* report in the *San Francisco Chronicle*, Feb. 2, 2014, p. D-2.

85. Lingling Wei & Carolyn Cui, "China is Seeking U.S. Assets", *Wall Street Journal*, May 20, 2013, online at: http://online.wsj.com/article/SB10001424127887324787004578494632401290050.html See also: "China to Use Forex Reserves to Finance Overseas Investment Deals", *Bloomberg News*, Jan. 14, 2013, online at: http://www.bloomberg.com/news/2013-01-14/china-to-use-forex-reserves-to-finance-overseas-investment-deals.html

86. "China Quietly Invests Reserves in U.K. Properties", *Wall Street Journal*, Feb. 24, 2013, online at: http://online.wsj.com/article/SB10001424127887323699704578323670119279066.html

87. Peter Coy, "Give Me Your Yuan", *Bloomberg Businessweek*, Aug. 5–11, 2013.

88. Ian Bremmer, president of the Eurasia Group, a consulting agency, quoted in Peter Coy, "Give Me Your Yuan", *Bloomberg Businessweek*, Aug. 5–11, 2013, p. 7.

89. "The future of Laos: A bleak landscape", *Economist*, Oct. 26, 2013, pp. 49–50. Online at: http://www.economist.com/news/asia/21588421-secretive-ruling-clique-and-murky-land-grabs-spell-trouble-poor-country-bleak-landscape

90. Ibid.

91. Jane Perlez and Bree Feng, "Laos Could Bear Cost of Chinese Railroad", *New York Times*, Jan. 1, 2013, online at: http://www.nytimes.com/2013/01/02/world/asia/china-builds-a-railroad-and-laos-bears-the-cost.html?_r=0

92. This photo of Laotian deforestation is from the *Economist* article cited in end note 89.

93. For a broader picture of the planned development of railroads in Southeast Asia see the Wikipedia entry Kunming–Singapore Railway at: http://en.wikipedia.org/wiki/Kunming%E2%80%93Singapore_Railway

94. Ibid.

95. See: "China pledges railway link to Nepal", *Phayul.com*, Sept. 11, 2013, online at: http://www.phayul.com/news/article.aspx?id=33976 and http://en.wikipedia.org/wiki/Lhasa%E2%80%93Shigatse_Railway [Shigatse (or Xigaze) is the second largest city in Tibet.]

96. Ananth Krishnan, "China is largest FDI source for Nepal, overtakes India", *The Hindu*, Jan. 26, 2014, online at: http://www.thehindu.com/news/international/world/china-is-largest-fdi-source-for-nepal-overtaking-india/article5618081.ece

97. "China, Nepal agree to deepen military ties", *The Hindu* [India], July 25, 2013.

98. Amos Irwin & Kevin P. Gallagher, "Chinese Investment in Peru: A Comparative Analysis", Dec. 2012, online at: http://ase.tufts.edu/gdae/Pubs/rp/DP34IrwinGallagherDec12.pdf

99. Fernando Menéndez, "The Trend in Chinese Investments in Latin America and the Caribbean", *China-U.S. Focus*, Dec. 19, 2013, online at: http://www.chinausfocus.com/finance-economy/the-trend-of-chinese-investments-in-latin-america-and-the-caribbean/

100. "Latin America playing a risky game by welcoming in the Chinese dragon", *Guardian*, May 30, 2013, online at: http://www.theguardian.com/global-development/poverty-matters/2013/may/30/latin-america-risky-chinese-dragon

101. Fernando Menéndez, op. cit.

102. Ibid.

103. Ibid.

104. Davies, K. (2013), "China Investment Policy: An Update", p. 4, OECD Working Papers on International Investment, 2013/01, OECD Publishing. http://dx.doi.org/10.1787/5k469l1hmvbt-en

105. Davies, K. (2013), cited earlier, p. 37 and elsewhere. As Davies notes, a major objective of the current (Twelfth) Five-Year Plan is "a move away from dependence on a massive trade surplus and capital inflows", which in turn is part of moving away (to some degree) from having a merely "export-oriented" economy.

106. For a recent discussion of local government debt in China see: "Local-government debt: Counting ghosts", *Economist*, Jan. 4, 2014, p. 32.

107. Ibid.

108. "China: The economy: A bubble in pessimism", *Economist*, Aug. 17, 2013, p. 39.

109. See for example "China 2013: A Year in Review with Shaun Rein", *China Briefing*, Jan. 7, 2014, online at: http://www.china-briefing.com/news/2014/01/07/china-2013-a-year-in-review-with-shaun-rein.html#sthash.Cr838QCY.dpuf

110. Davies, K. (2008), "China's Outward Direct Investment", in "OECD Investment Policy Reviews: China 2008", Nov. 7, 2008, p. 83, online at: http://www.oecd-ilibrary.org/finance-and-investment/oecd-investment-policy-reviews-china-2008/china-s-outward-direct-investment_9789264053717-5-en (Use the "read" option for free access.)

111. Davies, K. (2013), "China Investment Policy: An Update", cited earlier, p. 34.

112. Ibid., p. 35.

113. Ibid.; original source: Wen Jiabao, "Report on the Work of the Government", *XinhuaNet* website, March 15, 2011.

114. Ibid., pp. 37–38. Chen Deming was referring specifically to *non-financial* OFDI. If *financial* OFDI is included, the task of bringing OFDI into balance with IFDI is more difficult, because it is further out of balance at the present time.

115. This probably refers to annual inward and outward FDI *flows* rather than to accumulated stocks of inward and outward FDI. (The article was unclear on this point.) The complete balancing of total inward and outward FDI accumulated stocks may take a little longer. Ding Qingfen, "ODI set to overtake FDI 'within three years'", *China Daily*, May 6, 2011, online at: http://www.chinadaily.com.cn/business/2011-05/06/content_12457305.htm

116. The *China Daily* article cited above mentions a report by the U.S. Asia Society that also predicts that China's outward FDI is about to surge, and that the stock of outward FDI will likely reach between $1 and $2 trillion worldwide by 2020.

117. Nargiza Salidjanova, "Going Out: An Overview of China's Outward Foreign Direct Investment", U.S.-China Economic & Security Review Commission [of the U.S. government], *USCC Staff Research Report*, March 30, 2011, p. 11, online at: http://www.bioin.or.kr/upload/policy/1314079084656.pdf (accessed on June 26, 2013).

118. This of course is due to the fact that most outward FDI involves buying up existing companies, and thus automatically acquiring any technological knowledge and capabilities that they posses. One such study that shows this expected effect to actually exist is: Bruno van Pottelsberghe de la Potterie and Frank Lichtenberg, "Does Foreign Direct Investment Transfer Technology Across Borders?", June 2000, online at: http://www.ulb.ac.be/soco/solvay/cours/vanpottelsberghe/resources/FDI_REStat6874.pdf

119. Ibid., p. 10.

120. Even more surprising is the claim in a recent *New York Times* article that Malaysia has actually invested $2 billion more in Africa than China has. [See "Group of Emerging Nations Plans to Form Development Bank", March 26, 2013, online at: http://www.nytimes.com/2013/03/27/world/africa/brics-to-form-development-bank.html?_r=0&gwh=2F22632AC536A802E98BE22F3F756A6F] However, that investment is probably mostly to the Arab countries in north Africa, and China's impact on the continent as a whole, and to sub-Saharan Africa in particular, has been far greater than Malaysia's has been. And, as noted in the text, China's actual total economic penetration into Africa is much larger than it has been officially reported!

121. Xiaofang Shen, "How the private sector is changing Chinese investment in Africa", *Columbia FDI Perspectives*, #93, April 15, 2013, online at: http://www.vcc.columbia.edu/content/how-private-sector-changing-chinese-investment-africa This 2.2% figure for Chinese OFDI distribution to Africa is down from 4.1% in OFDI stock in Africa as of the end of 2010. (See Davies, K. (2013), cited earlier, p. 74.)

Besides the points mentioned in the text, there are also additional reasons to doubt that China's percentage of its outward FDI invested in Africa is as small as they claim. The United Nations Economic Commission for Africa says that Africa is attracting huge amounts of FDI, even (they say) "more FDI than any other continent", and that "By 2011, FDI projects in Africa grew by as much as 27%. In the first quarter of 2012 FDI inflows stood at USD80 billion and [are] projected to reach over USD150 billion in 2015." ["Celebrating a continent", May 27, 2013, available on the website http://www.uneca.org] Given that China is now universally recognized as the leading source of FDI in Africa, if these UN figures are correct China's outward FDI to Africa must be much bigger than they are claiming.

122. "Celebrating a continent", UN Economic Commission for Africa, op.cit.

123. Rob Minto, "Chart of the Week: Tracking China's Investments in Africa", *Financial Times*, April 30, 2013, online at: http://blogs.ft.com/beyond-brics/2013/04/30/chart-of-the-week-tracking-chinas-investments-in-africa/#axzz2afOiELhz

124. Xiaofang Shen, op. cit., originally calculated on the basis of data from the Chinese Ministry of Commerce as well as from data from each of the six examined host countries.

125. Susan L. Shirk, op cit., p. 135. Original source: *International Herald Tribune*, Nov. 3, 2006.

126. Quoted in Patrick Bond, "Obama in South Africa: Washington tells Pretoria how to 'play the game' in Africa", June 30, 2013, cited earlier.

127. "China's trade safari in Africa," *Le Monde Diplomatique*, May 2005.

128. Peter Wonacott, "In Africa, U.S. Watches China's Rise, Sept. 2, 2011, *Wall Street Journal,* online at: http://online.wsj.com/article/SB10001424053111903392904576510271838147248.html (accessed July 16, 2013).

129. French, Howard W. and Polgreen, Lydia, "Entrepreneurs from China Flourish in Africa", *New York Times*, Aug. 18, 2007, online at: http://www.nytimes.com/2007/08/18/world/africa/18malawi.html?em&ex=1187582400&en=7b8806ea0f69e210&ei=5087%0A&_r=1&&gwh=D992E60CC2D67ED0526C957807EF1164 (accessed July 16, 2013).

130. "Africa and China: More than minerals", *Economist*, March 23, 2013, online at: http://www.economist.com/news/middle-east-and-africa/21574012-chinese-trade-africa-keeps-growing-fears-neocolonialism-are-overdone-more (accessed July 16, 2013).

131. According to the Wikipedia entry on Africa-China economic relations, online at: http://en.wikipedia.org/wiki/Africa-China_economic_relations
This article notes that the Chinese diaspora in Africa has served to help facilitate the marketing of Chinese goods in Africa, and the promotion of investment from China.

132. "Africa-China Trade", *Financial Times*, Jan. 24, 2008, online at: http://media.ft.com/cms/e13530f4-c9df-11dc-b5dc-000077b07658.pdf Since this article is focusing on trade, some of these 800 Chinese corporations "operating in Africa" may have only been engaged in trading there; but many others also have growing stocks of FDI in Africa.

133. This map is taken from the Business Insider website at:
http://www.businessinsider.com/map-chinese-investments-in-africa-2012-8

134. "NGOs, weapons of 'populist/humanitarian' imperialism, now wielded by competing imperialists in the new scramble for Africa", *Frontlines of Revolutionary Struggle*, April 28, 2013, online at: http://revolutionaryfrontlines.wordpress.com/2013/04/28/ngos-weapons-of-populisthumanitarian-imperialism-now-wielded-by-competing-imperialists-in-the-new-scramble-for-africa/

135. Christopher Alessi & Stephanie Hanson, "Expanding China-Africa Oil Ties", *Council on Foreign Relations*, Feb. 8, 2012, online at: http://www.cfr.org/china/expanding-china-africa-oil-ties/p9557

136. Gregor Sahler, "China's crusade for African oil on the example of Sudan", document V181809, GRIN Verlag, 2010. See also, Robert I. Rotberg, ed., *China Into Africa: Trade, Aid and Influence* (Brookings Institute, 2008), for discussion of Chinese military aid to Sudan and China's role in Sudan's oil production.

137. Salil Tripathi, "The East India Company rides again: China's attitude to Africa has many of the hallmarks of old-fashioned European imperialism", *Guardian*, Nov. 15, 2006, online at: http://www.theguardian.com/business/2006/nov/15/businesscomment.india

138. Elissa Jobson, "Chinese firm steps up investment in Ethiopia with 'shoe city'", *Guardian* (U.K.), April 30, 2013, online at: http://www.theguardian.com/global-development/2013/apr/30/chinese-investment-ethiopia-shoe-city The article claims that this particular massive Chinese shoe company investment seems to be something different than "voracious neocolonial pillaging", however.

139. "China's role in Africa under scrutiny", *Bloomberg News* report, in *Business Report* (Zambia), June 9, 2013, online at: http://www.iol.co.za/business/international/china-s-role-in-africa-under-scrutiny-1.1529528#.Ufmc9axsjms For another article on this particular situation in Ghana, which shows how the ordinary Chinese miners have themselves been victimized by the companies that hired or recruited them, see: "Chasing a Golden Dream, Chinese Miners Are on the Run in Ghana", *New York Times,* June 10, 2013, online at: http://www.nytimes.com/2013/06/11/world/africa/ghana-cracks-down-on-chinese-gold-miners.html?pagewanted=all&_r=0

140. Xan Rice, "China's Economic Invasion of Africa", *The Guardian* (U.K.), Feb. 6, 2011, online at: http://www.theguardian.com/world/2011/feb/06/chinas-economic-invasion-of-africa

141. "China's role in Africa under scrutiny", *Bloomberg* report cited above.

142. Lydia Polgreen, "Group of Emerging Nations Plans to Form Development Bank", *New York Times*, March 26, 2013, online at: http://www.nytimes.com/2013/03/27/world/africa/brics-to-form-development-bank.html?_r=0

143. David Smith, op. cit.

144. Xan Rice, op. cit.

145. Claire Provost and Rich Harris, "China commits billions in aid to Africa as part of charm offensive", *Guardian* (U.K.), April 29, 2013, online at: http://www.

theguardian.com/global-development/interactive/2013/apr/29/china-commits-billions-aid-africa-interactive

146. Tania Branigan, "Domestic critics carp over extent of China's munificence towards Africa", *Guardian* (U.K.), April 29, 2013, online at: http://www.theguardian.com/global-development/2013/apr/29/china-critics-aid-package-africa

147. China even admits this to some partial degree: "[S]ince the early 1980s, China has stressed that its aid strategy is about co-operation and mutual benefit rather than philanthropy." From Tania Branigan, op. cit.

148. Jonathan Kaiman, "Africa's future leaders benefit from Beijing's desire to win hearts and minds: China's African aid programme aims to offer 18,000 government scholarships and train 30,000 Africans by 2015", *Guardian* (U.K.), April 29, 2013, online at: http://www.guardian.co.uk/global-development/2013/apr/29/africa-future-leaders-china-aid-programme

149. Tania Branigan, op. cit.

150. Geoff Dyer, *The Contest of the Century* (NY: Alfred A. Knopf, 2014), p. 10. Dyer is the former bureau chief in Beijing for the *Financial Times* newspaper (London).

151. Data in this chart is from the Stockholm International Peace Research Institute (SIPRI), and their spreadsheet of military expenditures for 172 different countries which is available online at: http://www.sipri.org/research/armaments/milex/milex_database/milex_database The percentage figures have been calculated by us from that data.

152. "Defence Spending: Squeezing the Pentagon", *Economist*, issue of July 6, 2013, online at: http://www.economist.com/news/united-states/21580460-wrong-way-cut-americas-military-budget-squeezing-pentagon Certainly it is possible that these particular "sequestration" cuts may still be reversed, at least in part. But this situation still shows the mounting pressures on the U.S. to trim its military spending, rather than try to match the constant increases in Chinese military spending.

153. Nick Simeone, "Hagel outlines budget reducing troop strength, force structure", *American Forces Press Service* (of the U.S. Dept. of Defense), Feb. 24, 2014, online at: http://www.defense.gov/news/newsarticle.aspx?id=121703

154. Maggie Ybarra, "Pentagon budget priorities continue trend of decreased funding for NATO: Decline in U.S. spending fits with European trend", *Washington Times*, Feb. 26, 2014, online at: http://www.washingtontimes.com/news/2014/feb/26/pentagon-budget-cuts-wont-bode-well-nato/?utm_source=RSS_Feed&utm_medium=RSS (Accessed Feb. 26, 2014).

155. Source: http://www.globalfirepower.com

156. For information about the DF-41 ICBM, see "Five Types of Missiles to Debut on National Day", *Xinhua News*, Sept. 2, 2009, online at: http://news.xinhuanet.com/english/2009-09/02/content_11982723.htm See also "Intercontinental Ballistic Missile" entry on Wikipedia at: http://en.wikipedia.org/wiki/ICBM

157. "Work under way on China's second aircraft carrier at Dalian yard", *South China Morning Post*, Jan. 19, 2014, online at: http://www.scmp.com/news/china/article/1408728/work-under-way-chinas-second-aircraft-carrier-dalian-yard

158. "The U.S. Navy's huge, nuclear-powered aircraft carriers—capital ships that have long dominated military planning and budgeting—are slowly becoming obsolete, weighed down by escalating costs, inefficiency and vulnerability to the latest enemy weapons." —David Axe, "After the Aircraft Carrier: 3 Alternatives to the Navy's Vulnerable Flattops", *Wired*, March 20, 2013, online at: http://www.wired.com/dangerroom/?p=105583

159. "Weaponry and espionage: A shot from the dark", *Economist*, Nov. 30, 2013, p. 58. Online at: http://www.economist.com/news/international/21590960-formidable-munitions-become-easier-conceal-and-use-west-intensifying-efforts

160. Ibid. This rocket-torpedo is manufactured by a Russian-owned company in Kyrgyzstan, and is known to be exported to other countries.

161. Jason Koebler, "Report: Chinese Drone 'Swarms' Designed to Attack American Aircraft Carriers: The Chinese are taking unmanned aerial vehicle development very seriously, according to a new report", *U.S. News & World Report*, March 14, 2013, online at: http://www.usnews.com/news/articles/2013/03/14/report-chinese-drone-swarms-designed-to-attack-american-aircraft-carriers

162. Edward Wong, "Hacking U.S. Secrets, China Pushes for Drones", *New York Times*, Sept. 20, 2013, online at: http://www.nytimes.com/2013/09/21/world/asia/hacking-us-secrets-china-pushes-for-drones.html?nl=todaysheadlines&emc=edit_th_20130921

163. Map from Jan Van Tol, et al., "AirSea Battle: A Point-of-Departure Operational Concept", published by the Center for Strategic and Budgetary Assessments, 2010, p. 14. The CSBA is an American ruling class think tank concerned with military issues and "focusing on matters of strategy, security policy and resource allocation".

164. Various sources for the information in this paragraph, including the Wikipedia article on the PLA Navy at: http://en.wikipedia.org/wiki/Chinese_Navy

165. See for example Christopher Bodeen, "Inside 'Unit 61398': Portrait of Accused Chinese Cyberspying Group Emerges", *Huffington Post*, Feb. 20, 2013, online at: http://www.huffingtonpost.com/2013/02/20/inside-unit-61398_n_2722356.html

166. "Three astronauts are blasted into space as China launches mission to orbit the Earth from a remote site in the Gobi desert", *Daily Mail* [U.K.], June 11, 2013, online at: http://www.dailymail.co.uk/news/article-2339641/Three-astronauts-blasted-space-China-launches-mission-orbit-Earth-remote-site-Gobi-desert.html#ixzz2VvTfx1W7

167. Ibid.

168. "China: Power and patriotism: Reaching for the Moon", *Economist*, Dec. 21, 2013, p. 68.

169. "China: Moon rover captivates many lunar scientists", *L.A. Times* report reprinted in the *San Francisco Chronicle*, Jan. 9, 2014, p. A3.

170. That is, depending upon whether the U.S. and other countries have the political willingness (and the financial necessity because of the economic crisis) to allow China to beat them to Mars.

The head of the China National Space Administration, Sun Laiyan, said in 2006 that China would soon be starting deep space exploration focusing on Mars, and that a Chinese unmanned probe to Mars might occur as soon as 2014. A crewed mission to Mars is also planned, but for quite some time later. [See the Wikipedia entry: http://en.wikipedia.org/wiki/Manned_mission_to_Mars]

171. See Wikipedia entry for "List of U.S. Military Bases" at: http://en.wikipedia.org/wiki/List_of_United_States_military_bases and "The Worldwide Network of U.S. Military Bases", *Global Research*, at: http://www.globalresearch.ca/the-worldwide-network-of-us-military-bases/5564

172. See the entry for "Military Keynesianism" in the Dictionary of Revolutionary Marxism.

173. David Yanofsky, "China surges to become the world's third-largest arms exporter", *Quartz* website, March 18, 2013, online at: http://qz.com/64083/china-surges-to-become-the-worlds-third-largest-arms-exporter/

174. David Yanofsky, ibid

175. For one recent article on this topic, and how China has undercut the U.S.'s exorbitant prices for missile systems even for close U.S. allies like Turkey, see: Edward Wong and Nicola Clark, "China's Arms Industry Makes Global Inroads",

New York Times, Oct. 20, 2013, online at: http://www.nytimes.com/2013/10/21/world/asia/chinas-arms-industry-makes-global-inroads.html?hp&_r=1%

176. From the Wikipedia article "Africa-China Economic Relations", online at: http://en.wikipedia.org/wiki/Africa-China_economic_relations (Accessed June 14, 2013.)

177. From the Wikipedia article "Africa-China Economic Relations", ibid.

178. Ibid.

179. Michael Metcalf, *Imperialism with Chinese Characteristics? Reading and Re-reading China's 2006 Defense White Paper*, Discussion Paper number 16, NI Press (of the National Intelligence University), Washington, D.C., September 2011. This 74 page paperback volume can be ordered in printed form via Amazon.com, but it is also available free in PDF format at: http://www.ni-u.edu/ni_press/pdf/Imperialism_with_Chinese_Characteristics.pdf

180. Dr. Chen Zhou is a researcher at the PLA Academy of Military Sciences, War Theory and Strategic Studies Department, and according to Michael Metcalf is "one of the most well-known PLA writers on Chinese military matters". [Metcalf, op. cit., p. 7.]

181. Chen Zhou, "An Analysis of Defensive National Defense Policy of China for Safeguarding Peace and Development", in Michael Metcalf, op. cit., p. 34.

182. Chen Zhou, quoted in Michael Metcalf, op. cit., p. 12.

183. Ibid., p. 12.

184. Ibid., pp. 13–14.

185. Ibid., p. 14.

186. Ibid., p. 14.

187. Ibid., pp. 14–15.

188. Chen Zhou, quoted in Michael Metcalf, op. cit., p. 15.

189. Chen Zhou, ibid., pp. 41–42.

190. Ibid., p. 42.

191. Chen Zhou, quoted in Michael Metcalf, op. cit., p. 19.

192. Ibid.

193. Michael Metcalf, op. cit., p. 20.

194. Ibid., pp. 21–22.

195. One of the most recent official defense white papers is entitled "The Diversified Employment of China's Armed Forces", issued in April 2013 by the Information Office of the PRC State Council, online in English at: http://eng.mod.gov.cn/TopNews/2013-04/16/content_4442750.htm

196. "Djibouti Welcomes China to Build a Military Base", an English translation of an article on the Chinese-language website of the *Global Times,* posted on March 11, 2013. http://www.chinaafricaproject.com/djibouti-welcomes-china-to-build-a-military-base-translation/

197. "PLA Navy to build overseas military bases?", *Defense Statecraft* website, March 25, 2013, at: http://defensestatecraft.blogspot.com/2013/03/pla-navy-to-build-overseas-military.html (accessed Feb. 18, 2014).

198. Original map printed circa March 2013 in the *International Herald Leader,* a Chinese state-run newspaper, together with a commentary advising the PLA Navy on where to build overseas naval bases in order to protect the Chinese energy line in the Indian Ocean area. Posted on the *Defense Statecraft* website (see link in endnote 197).

199. "Filipinos protest China's actions", *San Francisco Chronicle,* July 24, 2013, p. A-14.

200. Ibid.

201. Ibid.; Tom Phillips, "Philippine president compares China's expansion to Nazi Germany", *The Telegraph* [U.K.], Feb. 5, 2014, online at: http://www.telegraph.co.uk/news/worldnews/asia/china/10618722/Philippine-president-compares-Chinas-expansion-to-Nazi-Germany.html It should be noted that Benigno Aquino is perhaps the most prototypical comprador politician in the world today, and it is no wonder that he would raise the call of alarm against China in the most extreme way, and wildly call on "the West" (meaning the U.S.) to take on China before it is "too late".

202. For information on the competing claims and areas of control in the Spratly Islands, see the Wikipedia entry at: http://en.wikipedia.org/wiki/Spratly_Islands_dispute

203. Japan has very recently started to further increase its "security" forces around these islands, including scrambling fighter jets to threaten Chinese vessels. ("Japan increases security around disputed islands", AP report in the *San Francisco Chronicle,* Sept. 12, 2013, p. A4.)

204. "Philippines: Japan promises help in territory dispute with China", AP report, *San Francisco Chronicle,* July 28, 2013, p. A-6.

205. See for example: "Anti-Japan Protests Mount in China", *Wall Street Journal*, Sept. 16, 2012, online at: http://online.wsj.com/article/SB10000872396390443720204578000092842756154.html

206. Justin McCurry, "China lays claim to Okinawa as territory dispute with Japan escalates", *Guardian* [U.K.], May 15, 2013, online at: http://www.theguardian.com/world/2013/may/15/china-okinawa-dispute-japan-ryukyu

207. Luo Yuan, a two-star general in the PLA who raised the issue of the status of Okinawa and the Ryukyu island chain in the *People's Daily* did however add in an interview: "Let's for now not discuss whether [the Ryukyus] belong to China, they were certainly China's tributary state. I am not saying all former tributary states belong to China, but we can say with certainty that the Ryukyus do not belong to Japan." [Ibid.]

208. Mohan Malik, "Bordering on Danger: A Sino-Indian boundary dispute risks flaring up", *Wall Street Journal*, Oct. 15, 2009, online at: http://online.wsj.com/article/SB10001424052748704107204574474433189540954.html

209. Henry Kissinger quoted in the Wikipedia article on the Sino-Vietnamese war, online at: http://en.wikipedia.org/wiki/Sino-Vietnamese_War

210. Ishaan Tharoor, "After Fighting Over Mountains, India and China Lock Horns in the Indian Ocean", *Time/World*, May 16, 2013, online at: http://online.wsj.com/article/SB10001424052748704107204574474433189540954.html

211. "Chinese Navy Fights Piracy in Somalia", China.org.cn, Feb. 28, 2012, online at: http://www.china.org.cn/video/2012-02/28/content_24748561.htm

212. Photo from the article by Rahul Singh, "China's submarines in Indian Ocean worry Indian Navy", *Hindustan Times*, April 7, 2013, online at: http://www.hindustantimes.com/India-news/NewDelhi/China-s-submarines-in-Indian-Ocean-worry-Indian-Navy/Article1-1038689.aspx

213. See the Wikipedia article on neoconservatism, in the section on the 1990s, online at: http://en.wikipedia.org/wiki/Neoconservatism

214. John Barry, "A New Pacific Strategy: Washington is evolving a deterrence theory for China", *Newsweek*, May 7, 2001.

215. The official U.S. government website promoting this TPP free trade grouping is at: http://www.ustr.gov/tpp

216. The U.S. has the most frequent trade rows with China. But they frequently occur between Europe and China as well. One recent example was described in "EU-China trade—Outlook: cloudy", *Economist*, June 8, 2013, pp. 74–75.

217. See for example the article, "The China-ASEAN 'Diamond Decade'", *ASEAN Briefing* website, Sept. 9, 2013, online at: http://www.aseanbriefing.com/news/2013/09/09/the-china-asean-diamond-decade.html

218. See: "China Proposes New Silk Road Free Trade Zone", by *China Briefing*, Sept. 17, 2013, online at: http://www.china-briefing.com/news/2013/09/17/china-proposes-new-silk-road-free-trade-zone.html

219. See: "Corruption: China Turns the Screws on Multinationals", *Bloomberg Businessweek*, c. Sept. 20, 2013, pp. 16–17. Another of the many articles on this topic, this one focusing on the British pharmaceutical giant GlaxoSmithKline and its bribery and misdeeds in China as well as on the general Western excuse that corruption is endemic in China, is "GlaxoSmithKline in China: Bitter Pill", *Economist*, July 20, 2013, p. 56.

220. "The Sinodependency index: Declaration of Chindependence: For an American multinational, is exposure to China still a good thing?", *Economist*, July 20, 2013, p. 64.

221. "The Obama Administration's Pivot to Asia", *The Foreign Policy Initiative*, Dec. 13, 2011, video and text summary online at http://www.foreignpolicyi.org/content/obama-administrations-pivot-asia

222. "Military diplomacy: Not so warm and fuzzy", *Economist*, June 9, 2012, p. 49.

223. "Pivot to the Pacific? The Obama Administration's 'Rebalancing' Toward Asia", *Congressional Research Service*, March 28, 2012, online at: http://www.fas.org/sgp/crs/natsec/R42448.pdf

224. Jamil Anderlini, "How long can the Communist party survive in China?", *Financial Times*, Sept. 20, 2013, p. 7, online at: http://www.ft.com/intl/cms/s/2/533a6374-1fdc-11e3-8861-00144feab7de.html

225. Ibid.

226. "China: Power and patriotism: Reaching for the Moon", *Economist*, Dec. 21, 2013, p. 68.

227. Barbara Demick, "China's Xi Jinping appears more Maoist than reformer so far", *Los Angeles Times*, June 8, 2013, online at: http://www.latimes.com/news/nationworld/world/la-fg-china-xi-20130608,0,2308743.story [Of course the claim here that Xi Jinping is any sort of "Maoist" is totally absurd, and demonstrates a very bourgeois understanding on the part of the reporter as to what "Maoism" actually is.]

Kalikot Book Series

V.I. Lenin famously wrote that, "Without revolutionary theory there can be no revolutionary movement."

However, such a revolutionary theory adept to solving the theoretical problems faced by the contemporary revolutionary left has been largely unforthcoming or unavailable. Additionally, due to a prevalent Eurocentrism in North American and European radical traditions, books by or about Third World revolutionaries and their movements remain often unheeded and dismissed. Ignorance of these movements, their movements, and their organic intellectual production has not been entirely willful as the capacity to translate, publish, and distribute such materials in English has remained limited. Thus, their voices and experiences remain largely unknown to revolutionaries around the world.

Kalikot Book Series aims to fill that gap through translating, compiling and publishing books that have been previously unavailable to North American and European audiences. This book series hopes to publish the work of theoreticians and activists from around the world, not only the Third World, that advocate a wide variety of marginalized revolutionary politics. These are books that seek to serve as interventions into numerous complicated problems faced by the contemporary revolutionary left and to not only educate, but to help forge a revolutionary movement capable of the tasks before it.

email: dhruvj@gmail.com
web: http://kalikotbooks.wordpress.com

ALSO FROM KERSPLEBEDEB & KALIKOT

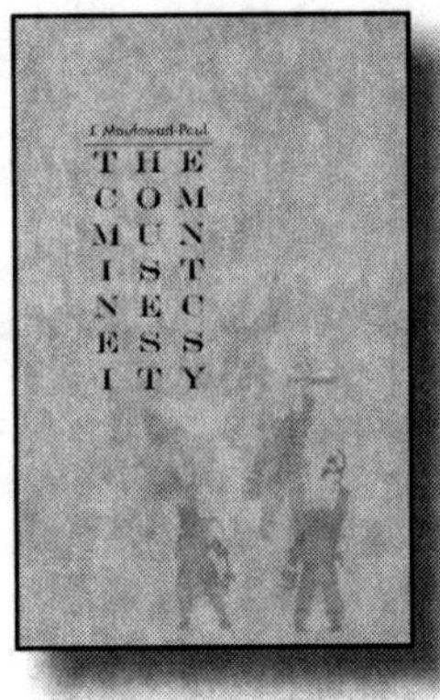

The Communist Necessity

J. Moufawad-Paul • 978-1-894946-58-2
168 pages • $10.00

A polemical interrogation of the practice of "social movementism" that has enjoyed a normative status at the centres of capitalism. Aware of his past affinity with social movementism, and with some apprehension of the problem of communist orthodoxy, the author argues that the recognition of communism's necessity "requires a new return to the revolutionary communist theories and experiences won from history."

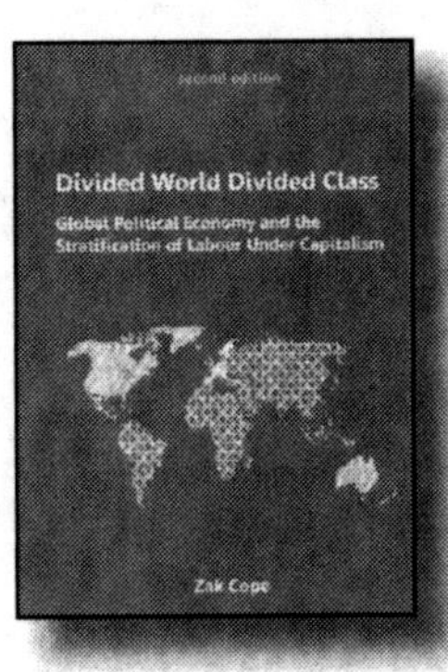

Divided World Divided Class: Global Political Economy and the Stratification of Labour Under Capitalism

SECOND EDITION

Zak Cope • 978-1-894946-68-1 • 460 pages • $24.95

This book demonstrates not only how redistribution of income derived from superexploitation has allowed for the amelioration of class conflict in the wealthy capitalist countries, it also shows that the exorbitant "super-wage" paid to workers there has meant the disappearance of a domestic vehicle for socialism, an exploited working class. Rather, in its place is a deeply conservative metropolitan workforce committed to maintaining, and even extending, its privileged position through imperialism.

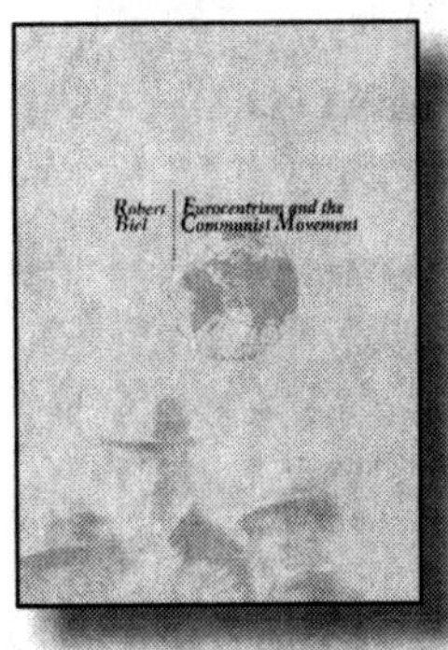

Eurocentrism and the Communist Movement

Robert Biel • 978-1-894946-71-1 • 215 pages • $17.95

A work of intellectual history, Eurocentrism and the Communist Movement explores the relationship between Eurocentrism, alienation, and racism, while tracing the different ideas about imperialism, colonialism, "progress", and non-European peoples as they were grappled with by revolutionaries in both the colonized and colonizing nations. Teasing out racist errors and anti-racist insights within this history, Biel reveals a century-long struggle to assert the centrality of the most exploited within the struggle against capitalism.

Settlers: The Mythology of the White Proletariat from Mayflower to Modern

J. Sakai • 978-1-62963-037-3
456 pages • $20.00

J. Sakai shows how the United States is a country built on the theft of Indigenous lands and Afrikan labor, on the robbery of the northern third of Mexico, the colonization of Puerto Rico, and the expropriation of the Asian working class, with each of these crimes being accompanied by violence. In fact, America's white citizenry have never supported themselves but have always resorted to exploitation and theft, culminating in acts of genocide to maintain their culture and way of life. This movement classic lays it all out, taking us through this painful but important history.

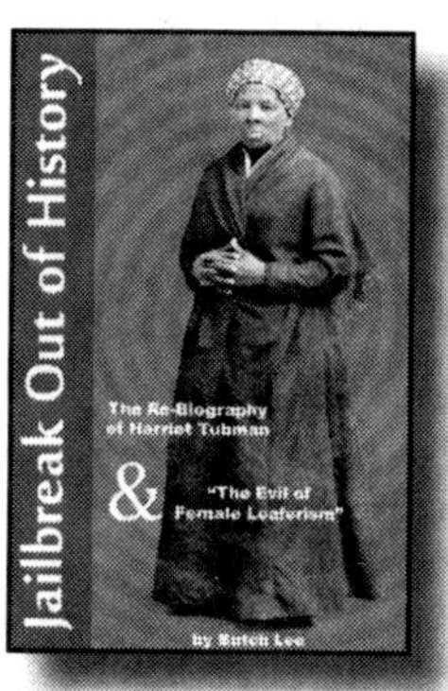

Jailbreak Out of History: the Re-Biography of Harriet Tubman

Butch Lee • 978-1-894946-70-4
169 pages • $14.95

The anticolonial struggles of New Afrikan/Black women were central to the unfolding of 19th century amerika, both during and "after" slavery. The book's title essay, "The Re-Biography of Harriet Tubman," recounts the life and politics of Harriet Tubman, who waged and eventually lead the war against the capitalist slave system. "The Evil of Female Loaferism" details the pivotal New Afrikan women's class struggles against capitalists North and South, and the creation of a neocolonial Black patriarchy, whose task was to make New Afrikan women subordinate to New Afrikan men just as New Afrika was supposed to be subordinate to white amerika.

Night-Vision: Illuminating War and Class on the Neo-Colonial Terrain

Butch Lee and Red Rover • 1883780004
187 pages • $14.95

bell hooks: "Night-Vision was so compelling to me because it has a spirit of militancy which reformist feminism tries to kill because militant feminism is seen as a threat to the liberal bourgeois feminism that just wants to be equal with men. It has that raw, unmediated truth-telling which I think we are going to need in order to deal with the fascism that's upon us." A foundational analysis of post-modern capitalism, the decline of u.s. hegemony, and the need for a revolutionary movement of the oppressed to overthrow it all.

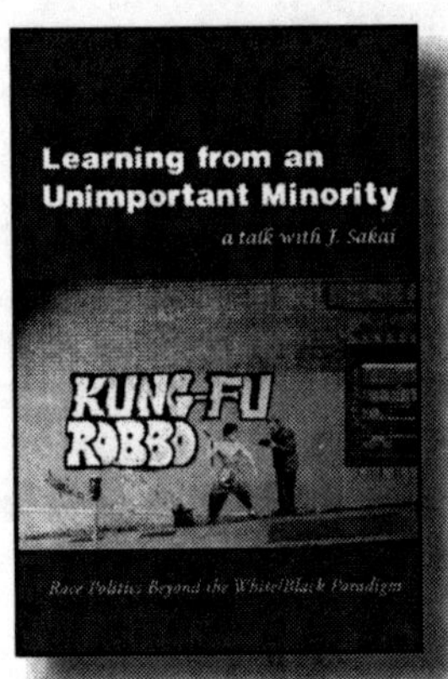

Learning from an Unimportant Minority: Race Politics Beyond the White/Black Paradigm

J. Sakai • 978-1-894946-60-5
118 pages • $10.00

Race is all around us, as one of the main structures of capitalist society. Yet, how we talk about it and even how we think about it is tightly policed. Everything about race is artificially distorted as a white/Black paradigm. Instead, we need to understand the imposed racial reality from many different angles of radical vision. In this talk given at the 2014 Montreal Anarchist Bookfair, J. Sakai shares experiences from his own life as a revolutionary in the united states, exploring what it means to belong to an "unimportant minority."

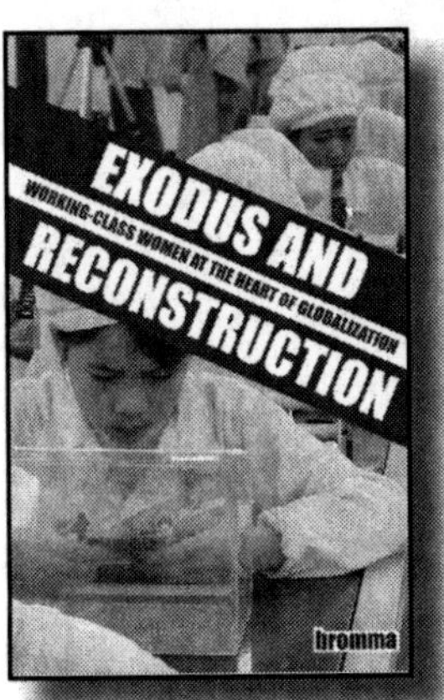

Exodus And Reconstruction: Working-Class Women at the Heart Of Globalization

Bromma • 9781894946421 • 37 pp. • $3.00

The decline of traditional rural patriarchy and the position of women at the heart of a transformed global proletariat. "At the most fundamental level, this politics is not about oil. It's not about religion. It's not about imperialist men versus anti-imperialist men. It's about women and women's labor: women at the heart of a transformed global proletariat."

The Worker Elite: Notes on the "Labor Aristocracy"

Bromma • 978-1-894946-57-5
88 pages • $10.00

Revolutionaries often say that the working class holds the key to overthrowing capitalism. But "working class" is a very broad category—so broad that it can be used to justify a whole range of political agendas. The Worker Elite breaks it all down, criticizing opportunists who minimize the role of privilege within the working class, while also challenging simplistic Third Worldist analyses.

KER
SPL
EBE
DEB

Since 1998 Kersplebedeb has been an important source of radical literature and agit prop materials.

The project has a non-exclusive focus on anti-patriarchal and anti-imperialist politics, framed within an anticapitalist perspective. A special priority is given to writings regarding armed struggle in the metropole, and the continuing struggles of political prisoners and prisoners of war.

The Kersplebedeb website presents historical and contemporary writings by revolutionary thinkers from the anarchist and communist traditions.

Kersplebedeb can be contacted at:

Kersplebedeb
CP 63560
CCCP Van Horne
Montreal, Quebec
Canada
H3W 3H8

email: info@kersplebedeb.com
web: www.kersplebedeb.com
www.leftwingbooks.net

Kersplebedeb